Native Son

The Emergence of a New Black Hero

Twayne's Masterwork Studies

Robert Lecker, General Editor

Native Son

The Emergence of a New Black Hero

Robert Butler

*Twayne Publishers * Boston*
A Division of G. K. Hall & Co.

Native Son: The Emergence of a New Black Hero
Robert Butler

Twayne's Masterwork Studies, No. 77

Published by Twayne Publishers
A division of G. K. Hall & Co.
70 Lincoln Street
Boston, Massachusetts 02111

Copyediting supervised by Barbara Sutton.
Book production by Gabrielle B. McDonald.
Typeset in Sabon
by Huron Valley Graphics, Inc., Ann Arbor, MI.

First published 1991.
10 9 8 7 6 5 4 3 2 1 (hc)
10 9 8 7 6 5 4 3 2 1 (pb)

Library of Congress Cataloging-in-Publication Data

Butler, Robert.
　　Native Son : the emergence of a new Black hero / Robert Butler.
　　　　p.　cm. — (Twayne's masterwork studies ; no. 77)
　　Includes bibliographical references and index.
　　ISBN 0-8057-8086-6 (hc). — ISBN 0-8057-8148-X (pbk)
　　　1. Wright, Richard, 1908–1960. Native son.　2. Afro-Americans in
literature.　3. Heroes in literature.　I. Title.　II. Series.
PS3545.R815N336 1991
　813'.52—dc20　　　　　　　　　　　　　　　　　　91-8827

For
my wife, Mary Jo,
and my children,
Becky, Geoff,
Mike, and Eric

Contents

Note on the References and Acknowledgments

All quotations from *Native Son, Black Boy,* and the pamphlet "How Bigger Was Born" are from the Perennial Classics paperback edition (New York: Harper & Row, 1966) and are cited parenthetically in the text.

I am grateful to Canisius College for granting me the sabbatical that provided the time and financial support necessary to research and write this book. My deepest thanks also go to my students at Tougaloo College and Stillman College who first opened my eyes to Wright's fiction and also to my students at Canisius College and Attica Correctional Facility who over the years have greatly deepened my knowledge of *Native Son.*

I would also like to thank Dean Walter Sharrow of Canisius College, Professor John Reilly of the State University of New York at Albany, and Professor Joe Weixlmann of Indiana State University for their steady support and encouragement.

I am grateful to Harper & Row Publishers for permission to quote from "How Bigger Was Born," *Native Son,* and *Black Boy.* My thanks also go to the editors of *Black American Literature Forum* for allowing me to use material from my articles on *Native Son.* Finally, I wish to thank Professor Keneth Kinnamon for so generously making available to me a prepublication copy of his *Essays on "Native Son."*

Richard Wright

Chronology: Richard Wright's Life and Works

1908	Richard Wright is born 4 September on a plantation outside Natchez, Mississippi, to Nathan Wright, a sharecropper, and Ella Wright, a country schoolteacher. He grows up in one of the most poverty-stricken and rigidly segregated parts of the South.
1914–1915	In search of better employment, the Wrights move to Memphis, Tennessee, where Nathan works as a night porter in a hotel and Ella works as a cook for a white family. The Wrights are left destitute when Nathan deserts Ella and the children for another woman. In 1915 Ella contracts an illness that eventually reduces her to the status of an invalid for the rest of her life.
1916–1918	Along with his mother and brother, moves to Jackson, Mississippi, to live with his maternal grandmother, Margaret Wilson, and then to Elaine, Arkansas, where they live with his aunt Maggie and her husband, Silas Hoskins. They are forced to leave Arkansas when Silas is murdered by whites who threaten to kill the entire family. For the next two years, the Wrights move back and forth between Helena and Jackson. During this time Wright's schooling is sporadic, and he becomes acutely aware of southern racism and violence, both of which leave indelible imprints on his consciousness and become important preoccupations in his fiction.
1918–1925	A period of serious and widespread racial discrimination against blacks and other minorities. The Ku Klux Klan is revived throughout the South and in various parts of the North, flourishing throughout the twenties. Racial rioting takes place in many American cities in the years immediately following World War I. Wright attends, with many interruptions, public and Seventh Day Adventist schools. In 1923 he enters the

Smith-Robertson Public School and in 1925 graduates valedictorian. Increasingly aware of southern racism and violence—brought to a sharp focus when the brother of a high school friend is murdered by whites—he decides to leave Mississippi. Saving enough money from an assortment of menial jobs, he arrives in Memphis, Tennessee, in November, 1925.

1926 Begins to read widely and is especially drawn to H. L. Mencken's ideas criticizing American society and modern life. At this point he also begins to read seriously such American naturalists as Theodore Dreiser, Sherwood Anderson, and Sinclair Lewis and is also strongly influenced by European realists like Henrik Ibsen, Emile Zola, and Fyodor Dostoyevski. His period in Memphis is a profound psychological awakening that transforms his life and confirms his desire to be a writer.

1927–1931 Moves to Chicago in December 1927 and shortly thereafter is joined by his mother and brother. After working as a waiter and helper in a grocery store, he passes a civil service examination and becomes a postal clerk, a job that enables him to work nights and spend his days reading and writing. Develops a strong interest in Edgar Allan Poe and also begins to read works by T. S. Eliot, Charles Baudelaire, André Gide, Thomas Mann, Friederich Nietzsche, Gustave Flaubert, and Nickolai Gogol. Soon after the stock market crash of 1929 he loses his position as a postal clerk and is forced to support himself and his family with a series of low-paying jobs; for much of this time he has no choice but to live in slum housing very much like that depicted in *Native Son*. In 1930 he becomes an aide at the South Side Boys Club, where he works directly with young men from Chicago street gangs. In 1931 he begins work with the Federal Negro Theatre and becomes a writer for the Illinois Writers' Project.

1932–1934 Becomes interested in Marxism, listening to Communist speakers in Washington Park and attending meetings of the John Reed Club, an organization of young writers committed to using literature as a tool for promoting Marxist ideas. Begins publishing poems, stories, and essays in *New Masses, Left Front,* and other leftist journals. Joins the Communist party in 1933.

1935–1936 Becomes widely known in Chicago literary circles and develops friendships with the novelists James T. Farrell and Nelson Algren. Begins work on his first novel, *Lawd Today,* in 1935 and publishes "Big Boy Leaves Home" in the *Negro Caravan* in 1936. By the end of the year he completes all four stories that would later be published in *Uncle Tom's Children* and begins work on *Native Son*.

1937　Has ideological differences with members of the Chicago John Reed Club and in the winter of 1937 moves to New York, where he becomes the Harlem editor of the *Daily Worker*. Keeping to a rigorous writing schedule, he works intensively on *Native Son* throughout the year.

1938　*Uncle Tom's Children* is published, making Wright one of the Communist party's outstanding young writers. He also becomes deeply interested in the Robert Nixon case, involving an 18-year-old black man accused of murdering a white woman. He does extensive research on the case and uses it as a documentary parallel to characters and events in *Native Son*.

1939　Wins a Guggenheim Fellowship, enabling him to work full-time on the completion of *Native Son*.

1940　*Native Son* is published on 1 March. Later in the year Wright collaborates with Paul Green on a stage version of the novel and begins work on *Twelve Million Black Voices,* a documentary study of the black South featuring photographs by Edward Rosskam.

1941　Receives the Spingarn Medal awarded by the NAACP to an outstanding Negro. Marries Ellen Poplar, a white woman, on 12 March despite her parents' strong objections to her marrying a black man. His doubts about being a member of the Communist party intensify, partly because of the party's turning away from American racial issues in order to pursue a broader struggle against fascism in Europe. Begins to feel sharply divided between his commitment to opposing racial injustice in America and his loyalty to party ideology.

1942　Officially breaks with the Communist party. *Twelve Million Black Voices* is published in October. He completes a manuscript version of *The Man Who Lived Underground,* a short novel notable for its existential rather than Marxist vision of life.

1943　Visits the Deep South to give a lecture at Fisk University in April; the trip reacquaints him directly with the problems of the segregated South, triggering his desire to write his autobiography. By the end of the year he has written *American Hunger,* an autobiography that covers his life up to his departure from Chicago in 1937.

1944　Wright's public disavowal of communism, "I Tried to Be a Communist," is published in the *Atlantic Monthly*.

1945   *Black Boy,* a shortened version of Wright's autobiography, covering his childhood and adolescence in the South, is published in March as a Book-of-the-Month Club selection. Later in the year he meets writer James Baldwin and helps launch Baldwin's career by assisting him in receiving a grant from the Eugene Saxton Foundation.

1946–1947   Decides to "exile" himself permanently in France, leaving the United States on 1 May 1946. His circle of friends in France includes such existentialists as André Gide, Jean-Paul Sartre, and Simone de Beauvoir, as well as American expatriate writers Gertrude Stein, Baldwin, and Chester Himes. He also develops close ties with the West Indian poet Aimé Césaire, the Jamaican writer George Padmore, and the African intellectual Léopold Senghor, each of whom is committed to viewing the situation of black people from a global, "third world" perspective.

1949–1950   Works intensively on a film version of *Native Son,* for which he writes the script and acts the lead role of Bigger Thomas.

1951–1956   Works on two novels, *The Outsider,* published in 1953, and *Savage Holiday,* published in 1954. Both novels reflect his increasing interest in French existentialism. In 1953 Wright visits the Gold Coast (now known as Ghana), where he observes firsthand an African nation in the process of liberating itself from colonial rule.

1955–1956   Participates in the Bandung Conference in Indonesia, which focuses on problems of the third world. His book *The Color Curtain* appears in March 1956 and places heavy emphasis on race as the crucial factor in resolving the problems of Western and third-world cultures. In September 1956 he helps organize the First Congress of Negro Artists and Writers in Paris.

1957–1958   Works on a new novel, *Mississippi,* as the first installment of a trilogy centering on a black man's experience in the South and his exile in France. The first volume appears in 1958 as *The Long Dream. White Man, Listen!,* a book about black culture and politics, is published in October 1957.

1960   Dies suddenly from a heart attack, on 28 November, while being treated for an unrelated illness in a Paris hospital.

Literary and Historical Context

1

Cultural Background

Like many American masterworks arising from realistic and naturalistic traditions, *Native Son* vividly reflects the history of its time. It is therefore important that its readers have a clear grasp of the specific historical events and trends that helped shape the novel. Three particular aspects of modern American history are crucial to an understanding of *Native Son:* the Great Migration of blacks from the rural South to the urban North in the first half of the twentieth century; the Great Depression, which produced a major crisis in American culture between 1929 and 1940; and the interest in radical leftist politics that developed in response to this crisis. As a glance at the Chronology of Richard Wright's life and works immediately makes clear, Wright personally experienced each of these three important aspects of modern American history and was thus able to write about them with special force and authority.

Historians August Meir and Elliott Rudwick describe the Great Migration as a pivotal event in Afro-American history: "After the Civil War and Emancipation, the major watershed in American black history was the Great Migration to Northern cities that began during

3

the First World War. According to the census of 1910, blacks were overwhelmingly rural and Southern; approximately three out of four lived in rural areas and nine out of ten lived in the South. A half century later Negroes were mainly an urban population, almost three-fourths of them being city dwellers. The changes in the texture of Negro life that have resulted are enormous."[1] Driven physically out of the South by agricultural disasters brought on by the boll weevil epidemic, soil depletion, and massive flooding, and also alienated from southern culture by its system of segregation, blacks flocked to northern cities in search of a better life. Between 1900 and 1910 the black population of New York grew by 51 percent and the black population of Chicago expanded by 30 percent. The years surrounding World War I witnessed an especially dramatic increase in the numbers of people living in northern cities, for the war greatly stimulated northern industry, creating an enormous need for both skilled and unskilled labor. Between 1910 and 1919 Chicago's black populace more than doubled in size, and it continued to grow steadily throughout the 1920s. Cleveland's black community grew from 8,000 in 1910 to 34,000 in 1919, and such cities as Detroit, Philadelphia, and Boston also witnessed dramatic increases in their black populations. Even though the Great Depression took away much of the economic lure of the northern city, the migration of blacks northward continued, although at a slower rate.

The immediate result of the Great Migration was a bitter disappointment for blacks, because their rapid infusion into northern cities soon produced teeming ghettos, such as the one depicted in *Native Son*. Rather than being integrated with the mainstream of northern life, where they could get a fair share of the tremendous prosperity in America brought on by World War I, blacks found themselves again segregated as second-class citizens. This segregating was done in a number of ways. On a personal level, blacks were kept out of white neighborhoods by violence directed at them in the form of beatings, stonings, and the bombing of their homes. White home owners also formed so-called neighborhood improvement associations for the purpose of excluding blacks, and real estate agencies like that owned by

Mr. Dalton in *Native Son* developed restrictive covenants that prevented blacks from renting apartments and buying homes in all-white sections of the city.

For people like Richard Wright and characters like Bigger Thomas, the problem was exacerbated because they migrated to Chicago at a time coinciding with the onset of the Great Depression. If racial discrimination made the northern city a harsh environment for blacks in the first quarter of the twentieth century, the widespread unemployment and economic deprivations brought on by the depression made city life even more difficult. And although unemployment rates during the depression were extraordinarily high for all Americans, they were even higher for blacks. By 1933 between 25 percent and 40 percent of blacks in major urban centers were on public assistance, a mode of life reducing them to the sort of marginal subsistence level depicted so powerfully in *Native Son*. In 1934 fully 38 percent of all black workers were "incapable of support in any occupation."[2] For the most part, the majority of black people who were able to get work during the depression could find only the kind of low-paying, dead-end jobs that would not keep them far above the bare subsistence level provided by public relief.

The response of many American intellectuals and artists to the widespread suffering brought on by the depression was to raise fundamental doubts about traditional American values and institutions and to commit themselves to radical left-wing politics promising a new order of things. Novelists like John Dos Passos, James T. Farrell, and John Steinbeck, unlike the apolitical writers of the twenties, produced an important body of literature that was deeply grounded in social issues and cried out for basic political, economic, and social change. Richard Wright, who became seriously interested in Marxist ideas in the early thirties and who formally joined the Communist party in 1933, saw his fiction as a "weapon" to be used in the struggle for transforming American society. *Native Son* was begun just three years after Wright became a Communist and was intended to be a radical indictment of the American system that Wright felt had been brought to the verge of collapse by the depression.

The importance of Wright's involvement with communism cannot be overemphasized, because it supplied him with what he would later call "the first total emotional commitment of my life," a new faith to replace the old beliefs shattered by the disappointments of the Great Migration and the shocks of the depression. Communism helped Wright develop as a man and as a writer, for it gave him a coherent philosophical vision, "an organized search for truth" that intellectually stabilized him in a world that seemed to be falling apart. It also gave him an imaginatively potent vision of human unity, "a common vision that bound us all together,"[3] which Wright needed for both his writing and his psychological well-being. Communism therefore endowed Wright with the same sense of identity it briefly supplied for Bigger Thomas, who toward the end of *Native Son* can feel stabilized "for the first time in his life" when Max's Communist vision helps him see "vague relations" between himself and others, leading to "a new sense of the value of himself " (334).

It is important to realize, however, that although *Native Son* was written while Wright was an active worker for the Communist party, the novel is much more than a propagandistic tract that oversimplifies human experience to promote Marxist ideas. While writing the novel Wright felt a healthy tension between his commitment to political ideology and his own sense of black American life arising from his personal experiences. Wright's novel thus enriches his personal outlook with a political vision that gives it unity, depth, and resonance, but at no point does political abstraction distort or compromise the integrity of what Wright as an individual black man knew. Wright's fierce devotion to portraying the realities of black life in America as he honestly felt them eventually created problems for him with the Communist party, from which he resigned in 1942, following several years of increasing doubt. He finally saw communism as depriving him of the independence and freedom he needed to reveal fully his vision of American black life. As he observed in *American Hunger,* communism ironically took on many of the repressive features of southern life against which he had earlier rebelled: "I had fled from men who did not like the color of my skin and now I was among men who did not like the color of my thoughts."[4]

Cultural Background

Alfred Kazin once described the thirties as a period that gave Americans "an education by shock."[5] *Native Son,* composed during the depths of this crucial decade, indeed provides its readers with a similar kind of "education." Written by a man who had directly experienced in his own personal life some of the decisive events and movements of modern American history, the novel is a remarkable mirror of its times. But Wright's masterwork is much more than a period piece providing dead footnotes to the past. Because Wright was a genuine artist, he was able to transform his record of his own era into a rich and compelling vision that transcended its times, addressing its readers in a universal way. *Native Son* therefore continues to "educate" us in shocking lessons that are as relevant today as they were in 1940.

2

The Importance of the Work

It is difficult even today to exaggerate the importance of Richard Wright's *Native Son*, a book that dramatically changed the ways in which American blacks and whites envision each other and represent themselves in literature. As Irving Howe has pointed out,

> The day *Native Son* appeared, American culture was changed forever. No matter how much qualifying the book might later need, it made impossible a repetition of the old lies. . . . Richard Wright's novel brought out in the open, as no one ever had before, the hatred, fear and violence that have crippled and may yet destroy our culture.
>
> A blow at the white man, the novel forced him to recognize himself as an oppressor. A blow at the black man, the novel forced him to recognize the cost of his submission.[6]

Like Whitman's *Leaves of Grass*, Twain's *Adventures of Huckleberry Finn*, Dreiser's *Sister Carrie*, and other seminal works in American literary tradition, *Native Son* emphatically brought something new into American consciousness. First, it boldly presented a new black hero who was radically different from any of his predecessors in formal literature. It also told this hero's story from a fresh literary point of view. And this point of view allowed Wright to dramatize the world of urban blacks as no previous writer had been able to, meticulously detailing the hard facts of ghetto life from an insider's perspective.

Certainly no serious account is made of the black urban masses in previous white literature of the American city. Although the city was given a great deal of attention in American literature after the Civil War and assumed a prominent position in American fiction during the twenties and thirties, none of the many urban novels written by whites during these times focus on black people in any sustained or meaningful way. William Dean Howells's novels, several of which were strongly committed to a "realistic" portrayal of the social classes in the late nineteenth-century American city, either contain no black characters or give very marginal status to blacks, with the "darky" who silently and invisibly tends the furnace in *The Rise of Silas Lapham* (1885). Even classic naturalistic novels, which were interested in revealing the harsher facts of American urban life, scarcely mention black people. Urban novels by Stephen Crane and Theodore Dreiser largely ignore blacks, and when blacks are noticed in books like James T. Farrell's *Studs Lonigan* (1935) they are vaguely described as an oncoming wave of intruders who will displace people from their ethnic neighborhoods.

Black fiction prior to *Native Son* is also noticeably lacking in detailed, realistic portraits of the impoverished masses of urban blacks. Although Charles W. Chestnutt lived for a considerable time in the urban North and wrote novels that can be considered "protest" novels, these books are set in the South and center on middle-class figures, such as Dr. Miller in *The Marrow of Tradition* (1901), or mulattoes aspiring to enter the white world, such as Rena Walden in *The House behind the Cedars* (1900). Paul Laurence Dunbar focused mainly on rural southern blacks who were content to avoid the corrupting influences of northern cities, and when he did write about urban blacks in *The Sport of the Gods* (1902) it was with considerable detachment and some disdain. James Weldon Johnson's *The Autobiography of an Ex-Colored Man* (1927) clearly expresses a preference for the city over the rural South; however, his city of preference is not a restrictive ghetto but a place of expanded possibility. Entering New York harbor, Johnson's middle-class protagonist envisions the city as an "enchanted spot," a place where he can rise in life. He condescendingly refers to poverty-stricken blacks as "the desperate class,"[7] and Johnson's novel provides only shadowy, oblique images of such people. Jean Toomer's *Cane* (1923) mainly tells the story of blacks living in the rural South, but when it does depict life in Washington, D.C., and Chicago it describes these cities in a lush, impressionistic manner, accentuating their poetic qualities. Claude McKay's *Home to Harlem* (1928) likewise stresses the black city's exotic qualities, envisioning it mostly as a place of freedom, excitement, and pleasure.

But *Native Son* speaks with a new voice, one that provides an intimate and shockingly realistic account of the plight of poor blacks in a massive ghetto. From the dissonant ringing of the alarm clock that opens the novel to the harsh clanging of Bigger's cell door that concludes the book, Wright jars us with a fresh novelistic voice that calls us to a sharp awareness of the ravaged world of America's urban blacks. Filtering the novel through not the cultured mind of an omniscient author but the highly charged consciousness of an uneducated and embittered black man who has been radically cut off from the mainstream of American life, Wright makes the novel's perspective something altogether new in American literature, a view of the ghetto from the standpoint of one of its victims.

Native Son is also an important work in American and Afro-American tradition because of its enormous influence on subsequent literature. The immediate impact of the book was to create what Robert Bone has called "the Wright School"[8] of fiction in black literature. Throughout the forties and early fifties younger black writers regarded *Native Son* as a paradigm and molded their own work along the thematic and formal lines established by Wright's masterwork. William Attaway's *Blood on the Forge* (1941), for example, imitated Wright's scrupulous naturalism in his story of black workers in Pennsylvania steel mills. Ann Petry's *The Street* (1946) owes much to Wright's depiction of the urban environment as a powerful force attacking the central character's basic aspirations. Willard Motley's *Knock on Any Door* (1947), although centering on a white protagonist named Nick Romano, follows the plot line of *Native Son* nearly point by point. Chester Himes's *If He Hollers Let Him Go* (1947) and Lloyd Brown's *Iron City* (1951) also show the strong influence of *Native Son* in their descriptions of the violent pressures of a racist urban environment on black individuals.

In a broader sense, *Native Son* has continued to influence black literature well beyond those who counted themselves among "the Wright School." Even though James Baldwin went to great lengths to make it clear that his muses were quite different from those which inspired Wright, Wright's brutally honest depiction of the relationships between sex, race, and violence helped free Baldwin to ground much of his own work in those preoccupations. Ralph Ellison's *Invisible Man* (1952) raises many of the same questions posed by *Native Son* even though it provides very different answers to those questions. Wright's example as a politically engaged writer who had a deep understanding of how the social environment affected individual black people inspired a whole generation of black activist writers of the sixties and seventies who read *Native Son* as a novel containing powerful "relevance" to their own situations. Claude Brown's *Manchild in the Promised Land* (1965), with its gritty description of Harlem life, is clearly cut from the same bolt of cloth Wright wove for *Native Son,* and Eldridge Cleaver in *Soul on Ice* (1968) characterizes himself as a native son moving in a direction Wright helped him define. Very recently, Clarence Major has listed *Native Son* as one of the novels that awakened him as a writer, and he described his first reading of the novel as "an overwhelming experience."[9]

Keneth Kinnamon has aptly observed that "with *Native Son* Wright became one of the important figures of twentieth century American fiction."[10] Wright's masterwork revolutionized American literature because it was courageous enough to attack old taboos that previous writers dared not approach and because it created startling new images about black experience that continue to inspire writers and disturb readers.

3

Critical Reception

The critical response to *Native Son* can be roughly divided into four main phases: the initial reviews, reactions to the novel from the forties to the midsixties, reassessments of the book from the midsixties to the late seventies, and continued reassessments in the eighties and nineties. From its publication in 1940 to the present, *Native Son* has sparked a vigorous critical debate involving a wide variety of critics who have approached the novel from many revealing perspectives.

The reviews of *Native Son* capture two crucial truths about the book: (1) the importance of the novel as a landmark work in American literature and (2) the immense controversy it evoked among a broad range of readers. The immediate impact of the book is evidenced not only by the intensity of its early reviews but also in the remarkable early sales. A Book-of-the-Month Club selection, the novel in its first printing was sold out within three hours of publication, and nearly 250,000 copies of the book were bought within six weeks.

Those reviewers who praised the book saw it as a seminal novel that promised to change the direction of American literature because it offered a new and disturbing view of the experience of blacks in America. Margaret Wallace, writing for the *New York Sun* a few days after the novel's appearance, sensed "a peculiar vitality" in the the book and argued that it was likely "to father other books" (5 March 1940). Henry Seidel Canby, writing for *Book-of-the-Month Club News,* boldly asserted that *Native Son* was "the finest novel written by an American Negro," a book so deeply grounded in black American experience that "only a Negro could have written it" (February 1940).

Most of the reviewers who praised the book saw in it a new kind of central character, one whose story provided a fresh perspective on black life in America. Milton Rugoff, in the *New York Herald Tribune Review of Books,* stressed that the "first extraordinary aspect of *Native Son* is that it approaches the tragedy of race not through an 'average' member but through a criminal" and that such a character is skillfully probed by Wright to "connect one individual's pathology to the whole tragedy of the Negro spirit in a white world" (3 March 1940). Sterling Brown's *Crisis* review two months later described *Native Son* as a "literary phenomenon" because it was the first novel about American blacks that provided a "psychological probing of the consciousness of the outcast, the disinherited, the generation lost in the slum jungles of American civilization" (June 1940).

Some leftist critics, such as Samuel Sillen, praised the book for its "revolutionary view of life" and its portrayal of the hero's "emancipatory" struggles against a society intent on crushing him (*New Masses,* 5 March 1940). Several other reviewers were struck by the novel's extraordinary impact, its power to transform the reader's consciousness. May Cameron saw *Native Son* as an "intense and powerful" novel that moved with "tremendous force and speed" to shock the reader into a new awareness of the position of blacks in American society (*New York Post,* 1 March 1940). Henry Hansen observed that Wright's novel "packs a tremendous punch, something like a big fist through the windows of our complacent lives" (*New York World Telegram,* 2 March 1940).

But many reviewers were equally vigorous in their condemnation of the book. One day after its publication, Howard Mumford Jones strongly attacked *Native Son* on aesthetic grounds, describing its plot as melodramatic and its themes as "dull propaganda" (*Boston Evening*

Transcript, 2 March 1940). Burton Rascoe's review for *American Mercury* sharply criticized the initial positive reviews and concluded, "Sanely considered, it is impossible for me to conceive of a novel being worse" (May 1940). And Clifton Fadiman assessed Wright as something less than a "finished novelist," pointing out that *Native Son* suffered from a melodramatic plot and "paper-thin" characters (*New Yorker,* 16 March 1940).

A number of other reviewers faulted the book for a lack of realism, claiming that its vision of American life was overdrawn and unfair. David Cohn, for example, described *Native Son* as "a blinding and corrosive study in hate" and argued vehemently that the condition of blacks in America was considerably better than the book would allow (*Atlantic Monthly,* May 1940). David Daiches maintained that the novel failed in its attempt to be an "illustrative fable" of actual race relations in America because Bigger's violent actions are too extreme for him to be a representative figure. Alleging that "Mr. Wright is trying to prove a normal thesis with an abnormal case," Daiches felt that *Native Son* deteriorated into melodrama that destroyed its realism (*Partisan Review,* May–June 1940).

On an even more serious level, some reviewers sharply questioned Wright's conception of Bigger Thomas, arguing that the character actually reinforced the brutal stereotypes the author wanted to destroy. Reverend Joseph McSorley argued in *Catholic World* that Bigger Thomas was "a savage moron" whose portrayal had the unintended effect of "spreading and deepening distrust of the Negro" (May 1940). Jonathan Daniels likewise concluded that "the story of Bigger Thomas is the story of a rat," a dehumanized figure used by the writer to develop his political "tract" (*Saturday Review of Literature,* 2 March 1940).

This extraordinary flurry of reviewing, which took place over a very brief period of four months after the novel appeared, laid the groundwork for much of the critical debate that would develop over the next fifty years. Indeed, most of the following questions raised by the early reviewers have continued to dominate discussions of the novel:

- Is the novel an artistic success, or is it crude propaganda that is deeply flawed by the melodramatic action and stereotyped characterization required by the advancement of a political thesis?
- Does the book supply a believable vision of race relations in America?
- Does it provide an accurate image of Afro-American life?
- Is the central character a boldly conceived new hero, or is he an overdrawn, heavily exaggerated, symbolic monster?

Much of the subsequent discussion of *Native Son* returns repeatedly to these questions, and different critics in different periods have responded to these questions in a great variety of ways.

The critical commentary on *Native Son* from a few years after its publication to the midsixties, however, was generally negative in its reply to these questions. This negativity can be explained by the general decline of naturalism as a literary mode in favor of less doctrinaire, more expressive fictional styles and also by a pervasive disenchantment with leftist politics after World War II. In addition, a perceived improvement in race relations after the war and a hope for the rapid integration of blacks with the mainstream of American life produced a desire for a more "universal," less "race conscious" type of literature that would speak to the needs of a multiracial audience. William Gardner Smith, for example, urged the Afro-American novelist to move away from "propaganda" and toward an art centered in "universal" themes, and he especially warned black writers to avoid making their characters "an exaggerated Bigger Thomas with all the stereotyped characteristics three times over."[11] Hugh Gloster, who admired *Native Son* as "a masterpiece of proletarian fiction," nevertheless felt that such writing was too restrictive for the post–World War II Negro writer. Gloster faulted Wright for looking at American reality from too limited a perspective: "He sees only a segment of life, and even this limited part he views in its most violent and horrible aspects."[12] James Baldwin and Ralph Ellison put the case against Wright most pointedly in widely read essays that seriously diminished Wright's literary reputation. Baldwin in "Many Thousands Gone" argued that "protest" novels like *Native Son* were intended to advance the cause of racial justice for American blacks but ironically had the reverse effect because they were populated by one-dimensional characters who reinforced all the stereotypes that trapped blacks in limited roles. He claimed that Bigger was a "monster created by the American republic" and a "social symbol revelatory of social disease,"[13] rather than a fully developed, realistic character who could adequately reflect the richness of Afro-American experience. Ellison in "The World and the Jug" and in interviews later collected in *Shadow and Act* likewise claimed that *Native Son* was artistically crude and that its vision of black life was too narrow because it was filtered through Bigger's limited perspective and Wright's excessive commitment to Marxist ideology.

One of the few major critics to come to Wright's defense during this period was Irving Howe, who in "Black Boys and Native Sons" sharply criticized the assessment of Wright made by Baldwin and Ellison. Howe argued that *Native Son* brought to a culmination the vital tradition of protest in black literature and chided Baldwin and Ellison for abandoning this tradition. He praised *Native Son* for its "superbly aggressive" tone, "apocalyptic" mood, and "clenched militancy" (Howe, 65, 69).

If this phase of criticism of *Native Son*, ranging from the early forties to the midsixties, provided a largely negative assessment of the novel, the next period of critical evaluation was almost uniformly positive. From the midsixties to the late seventies commentary on *Native Son* established it as a major American novel. Part of the reason for this development, of course, was the increasing militancy of the civil rights movement and a new interest in "black power," a phrase Wright himself had coined. Whereas post–World War II critics were likely to view Wright's aggressive politics as an asethetic liability, critics from the midsixties onward, especially those connected with the black arts movement, saw him as a model of the politically engaged writer. And while earlier critics were inclined to see Bigger Thomas disapprovingly as a dangerous stereotype of the "bad nigger," critics now were apt to hail Bigger as a prototype of the revolutionary black hero. Likewise, Wright's graphic portrayal of violence, which to critics like Baldwin was gratuitous and melodramatic, was to a newer generation of scholars a necessary part of Wright's vision of race relations in America.

Probably the work that most vividly illustrates this shift in sensibility is Eldridge Cleaver's "Notes on a Native Son," published in *Soul on Ice* (1968). Cleaver sharply criticized writers like Baldwin for ignoring the sociology of black experience and praised Wright for the depth of his social and political vision. Wright's political commitments to Marxism and black nationalism were viewed by Cleaver as artistic advantages, for they enabled him to envision more fully the condition of twentieth-century black people. Accordingly, Bigger becomes for Cleaver someone very different from the pathological monster Baldwin saw; on the contrary, he is regarded as "the black rebel of the ghetto and a man."[14] Edward Margolies's *Native Sons* (1968) likewise describes Bigger as a revolutionary figure rather than a sociological case study. Arthur P. Davis's *The Dark Tower* (1974) and Addison Gayle's *The Way of the New World* (1975) are later studies that also make a strong link between Bigger Thomas and the tradition of black activism.

This dramatic reassessment of Wright as a social and political thinker led to an equally dramatic reevaluation of him as an artist. From the midsixties onward, much was writtten to challenge the earlier view that Wright was a "powerful" but artistically inept writer, and *Native Son* was the focus of the majority of these studies. George E. Kent in 1969 observed that Richard Wright "seems now all too prophetic, all too relevant, majestically waiting that close critical engagement which forms the greatest respect that can be paid to a great man and writer."[15] In the years that followed, Wright's books, especially *Native Son,* received in scores of articles and books the "close critical engagement" it deserved and for so long had been deprived of.

One of the best critical studies to appear at this time was Donald Gibson's "Wright's Invisible Native Son." Submitting *Native Son,* and especially book 3, to a close and sensitive reading, Gibson argued that critics who regard Bigger as a stereotyped monster fail to *see* the inward, personal self buried underneath Bigger's public mask. By the end of the novel, Bigger can transcend his outward environment and through "solitary hours of minute introspection and self analysis" become a "private, isolated human" who is able to "face the consequences" of his life.[16] Dan McCall's *The Example of Richard Wright* (1969) is another penetrating study that first describes the extraordinary hatred and violence of the world Wright experienced as an American black man and then raises the crucial question, "How does one write about such a world and how is it to be interpreted in literary art?" Part of the answer is Wright's conscious desire in writing *Native Son* to move away from a dogmatically "realistic" style of fiction, with its emphasis on carefully depicting surface reality, and to use what McCall calls "psychodrama," a mode of fiction in the gothic tradition of Poe and Hawthorne that distorts outer reality as a way of dramatizing the mind through symbolism. Using this surrealistic technique, Wright was able to go to 'the center of the racial nightmare" as no previous writer had been able to. Bigger Thomas emerges from McCall's critical study as an archetypal rather than a stereotypical figure, a "legendary figure of the Western mind" who successfully embodies "the Myth of Race" just as figures like Robinson Crusoe embodied "the Myth of Individual Enterprise."[17]

McCall's book was followed three years later by another crucial study, Keneth Kinnamon's *The Emergence of Richard Wright* (1972). Kinnamon's discussion of *Native Son* stresses its roots in Wright's own experiences as well as the murder trial of Robert Nixon, a Chicago black man who was executed in 1938 for killing a white woman. He emphasizes, however, that Wright transformed actual experiences, adapting them for the purposes of his art. Carefully discussing the novel's structure, point of view, characterization, and symbolism, Kinnamon argues that each technique is artfully integrated to give full expression to "the theme of rebellion" that is the "central meaning of *Native Son*." Although he admits that the novel is not without flaws, most notably an "uneveness in style" and a less-than-satisfactory book 3, Kinnamon finally assesses *Native Son* as not only "a major document of the American racial dilemma" but also a book whose "art makes it . . . an important American novel" (Kinnamon, 143).

Three influential studies of the cultural background of Wright's fiction also emerged during this time. Blyden Jackson's biographical essay entitled "Richard Wright: Black Boy from America's Black Belt and Urban Ghettos" appeared in a 1969 special issue of *CLA Journal* devoted to Wright. Jackson placed Wright's fiction firmly in the context of his experience "deep within the world of the folk Negro," claiming that although Wright chose to live his adult life outside the South, his work is grounded in southern culture, which was both his "heart's home" and his "mind's tether."[18] George E. Kent's "Richard Wright: Blackness and the Adventures of Western Culture" appeared in the same special issue but approached Wright from another perspective, arguing that Wright's vision is centered in a broader context, his ambivalent response to the West. Kent sees Wright attracted in some ways to Western culture because of its tradition of Enlightenment rationalism that promises political freedom to oppressed people, but he also argues that Wright was deeply suspicious of other aspects of the West, especially its history of racism. Kent envisions Bigger Thomas as caught between these two opposite qualities of Western culture, for he both is victimized by Western racism and also achieves selfhood in a very Western way through "revolutionary will, individualism and self consciousness" (Kent, 341). Houston Baker, like Jackson, examines Wright's work in the context of black folk culture. His chapter on Wright in *Long Black Song* (1972) presents *Native Son* as a landmark work in American literature because it is the first novel to capture adequately the full force and richness of black folk experience. Baker draws revealing parallels between Bigger Thomas and trickster heroes like Brer Rabbit, bad-man heroes like Stackolee, and revolutionary figures like Nat Turner.

From the late sixties to the beginning of the eighties no less than four biographies of Wright were published. But by far the best biography for literary purposes is Michel Fabre's *The Unfinished Quest of Richard Wright* (1973), the product of nearly a dozen years of research and writing. Fabre's book sheds much revealing light on *Native Son*, not only for its detailed and accurate account of Wright's life prior to writing the novel but also because of its careful description of the circumstances surrounding the actual composition of the book, from 1937 to 1940. Wright's reading at this time is described, and the importance of his friendship with novelists Ralph Ellison and Nelson Algren is also stressed. Moreover, by comparing various drafts of the book, Fabre gives valuable insights into the technical decisions Wright made while writing the novel.

The period between the late sixties and the end of the seventies also produced a number of important scholarly articles on *Native Son*. Several focused sharply on the novel's intricate patterns of imagery. James A. Emmanuel's "Fever and Feeling: Notes on the Imagery of Native Son" (1968) studies images of light, darkness, walls, and erasure, arguing convincingly that such images are Wright's way of dramatizing Bigger's subconscious and conscious minds. James Nagel's "Images of Vision in *Native Son*" (1969) carefully explores how Wright used ocular images to suggest how Bigger's social world fails to see him as a human being and how Bigger is also beset with "blindness" when attempting to visualize himself and his environment. Robert Felgar's "The Kingdom of the Beast: The Landscape of *Native Son*" (1974) focuses on animal imagery, arguing that Wright employs it effectively as a way of defining the white world's stereotypical vision of the black world.

Several excellent comparative studies also emerge in this period. Keneth Kinnamon's "Richard Wright's Use of *Othello*" (1969) points out a number of significant parallels between Wright's novel and Shakespeare's play. Stephen Corey's "The Avengers in *Light and August* and *Native Son*" (1979) compares William Faulkner's Percy Grimm with State Attorney Buckley from *Native Son,* demonstrating that both figures are used by their authors to portray the hatred and power of the white world. The most revealing comparative study, however, is Yoshinobu Hakutani's "*Native Son* and *An American Tragedy:* Two Different Interpretations of Crime and Guilt" (1979), which makes a number of subtle distinctions between Wright and Dreiser that were ignored by many earlier critics. Hakutani's analysis stresses that, however similar the two novels are in general situation, they are crucially different in structure and theme.

Strong interest in *Native Son* continues in the 1980s and 1990s, although with not quite the same emphasis as in the preceding four decades. The focus of attention on the novel has shifted somewhat, with studies of Wright's political vision diminishing and analyses of his craftsmanship and literary sources increasing. Less is heard about Bigger as a revolutionary figure, and more is written about him as an existential hero, a tragic figure, or a modern antihero. The great majority of scholars and critics during this period are in general agreement about the artistic merit of *Native Son* and its importance as a major novel in American literature, although some reappraisal of a negative sort has also developed, especially among critics expressing dissatisfaction with Wright's portrayal of female characters.

Robert Felgar's *Richard Wright* (1980) asserts that Wright's fiction is "the most powerful to emerge to date in black literature." Felgar provides an antiheroic view of Bigger, claiming that he is a "monster" whose "life has not meant anything."[19] Jerry Bryant's "The Violence of *Native Son*" (1981) does a better job of exploring the novel's complexities because it makes a crucial distinction between Bigger's monstrous acts of violence and Wright's humane conception of the character. Agreeing with Felgar that Bigger is anything but a black activist hero, Bryant nevertheless insists that "he is not the brute of the newspaper stories."[20] Instead, Bryant sees Bigger as a "representative modern man" who is threatened by a dehumanizing social system but who, like Albert Camus's Meursault, can achieve a human identity through self-awareness. Michael Cooke's chapter on Wright in *Afro-American Literature in the Twentieth Century* (1984) likewise claims that while Bigger's self-destructive outer action leads to "self cancellation," his inner growth results in existential "self avowal," leading to his becoming "a participant in the life of the spirit."[21] This growth finally puts him on the verge of reconciliation with fellow human beings, a process tragically aborted when he is executed.

Joyce Ann Joyce's *Richard Wright's Art of Tragedy* (1985) examines Wright's craftsmanship in *Native Son,* analyzing his meticulous use of language and rhetorical strategies. Her careful study of the novel's style reveals that Bigger Thomas is not a naturalistic victim but a tragic hero. Bernard Bell's *The Afro-American Novel and its Tradition* (1987), however, takes a decidedly negative view of Wright and

Native Son, raising once again most of the objections made by Baldwin and others years earlier. Bell accuses Wright of drawing too bleak and narrow a picture of Afro-American life, neglecting the positive values that emerge from black community life and culture. He also agrees with Baldwin's aesthetic criticism of the novel, claiming that it suffers from melodramatic plotting, heavy-handed symbolism, and stereotypical characterization.

But the most serious recent complaints about *Native Son* come from critics expressing concern over the way Wright portrays female characters. Calvin Hernton, for example, in "The Sexual Mountain and Black Women Writers" used *Native Son* as an illustration of his thesis that "the complexity of black female experience has been fundamentally ignored" in modern black literature. In particular, he objects to Wright's portrayal of Bigger's mother and sister as "nagging bitches" and his depiction of Bessie as "a pathetic nothing."[22] Barbara Johnson likewise objects to a "careless misogyny"[23] in *Native Son,* claiming that Wright excuses Bigger's violence toward women by implying that white society forces Biggger into such actions. And Joseph Skerrett's "Composing Bigger: Wright and the Making of *Native Son,*" while generally sympathetic to Wright, nevertheless concludes that much of the violence in the novel is rooted in Wright's repressed resentment and hostility toward women.

Maria K. Mootry puts the case most strongly in "Bitches, Whores, and Woman Haters: Archetypes and Typologies in the Art of Richard Wright." Surveying all of Wright's major fiction but centering on *Native Son,* Mootry demonstrates that Wright's work expressed a crude macho ethic that is "brutal and unfair to women." Mootry claims Wright portrays Mary Dalton as the "bitch goddess of American success," Bessie as a mindless whore, and Mrs. Dalton as a suffocating mother who embodies the demands of a racist society. Because of Bigger's inability to see women as human beings and to form human relationships with them, he is trapped by a "narcissism" that restricts his growth and plunges him into self-destructive violence.[24]

Native Son thus flourishes as a work of art because it continues to inspire a wide range of deeply felt responses, reflecting its persistent ability to explore American reality in vigorous, disturbing ways. The controversy ignited by the book's publication in 1940, and debates that flamed throughout the forties, fifties, sixties, and seventies, burn brightly today. Wright, who saw the novel as a weapon to be used in the never-ending battle for social equality and who also envisioned art as participating in a ceaseless dialectic for truth, would surely be pleased by the knowledge that his masterwork continues to engage its readers in such vital, compelling ways.

A Reading

4

Introduction

As many critics and biographers have revealed, *Native Son* is deeply rooted in its author's personal life and the times in which he lived. Wright underscored this important point in "How Bigger Was Born" when he observed, "The birth of Bigger goes back to my own childhood and there was not just one Bigger but many of them, more than I could count" (viii). Indeed, the fictional life of Bigger Thomas was modeled not only after Wright's own direct experience but also on the lives of many black men he knew in both the South and the North. Consequently, much of the plotting of the novel came easily for Wright because "life had made the plot over and over again to the extent that I knew it by heart" (xxviii). It is therefore not surprising that Wright was strongly influenced by realism and naturalism, literary modes that are committed to recording faithfully the meaning and texture of actual life. As he remarked in *Black Boy*, "All my life had shaped me for the realism, the naturalism of the modern novel and I could not read enough of them" (274). Eagerly devouring books by European writers like Émile Zola, Gustave Flaubert, Henrik Ibsen, and Fyodor Dostoyevski as well as American writers like Sinclair Lewis, Sherwood Anderson, and Theodore Dreiser, Wright regarded realism and naturalism as powerful lenses through which he could better see himself and his world. Such writing not only gave him a way of honestly rendering his own experiences because it "opened up new avenues of seeing and feeling" but also connected him with a vital tradition of protest that empowered him with "weapons" he could use to speak out against a social world intent on victimizing American blacks (272).

Wright's attraction to naturalism as a literary style and a vision of life was particularly strong, for it seemed exactly the right literary mode for him to express his own painful experience. His selection of naturalism was not therefore the ideologically self-conscious choice it was for novelists like Frank Norris, John Dos Passos, or John Steinbeck, each of whom came from upper-middle-class backgrounds far removed from the harsh realities of the naturalistic universe wherein environment is always a brutal threat to the individual. Rather, Wright's attraction to naturalism arose from his instinctive recognition that his own life as an American black man was so closely mirrored in the naturalistic fiction he so hungrily devoured. As Houston Baker has pointed out, "Comparing Wright's life with almost any of Emile Zola's protagonists, one immediately recognizes the similarity. Wright's existence in the Black Belt and the urban ghettos of America was one in which events seemed predetermined by heredity . . . and the environment seemed under divine injunction to destroy."[25] Naturalism for Wright, then, was more than a set of literary conventions and procedures; it was something that gave him "a sense of life itself" (BB, 274), a vital and coherent rendering of his own disturbing experiences and the equally disturbing times in which he lived.

Naturalism was useful to Wright in a number of specific ways. First, it gave him a literary style that was a valuable tool for honestly probing the world around him. Inspired by Zola's notion that the writer was a kind of photographer or social scientist who carefully observed and recorded phenomena rather than romantically idealizing life, Wright was able to use a naturalistic style to objectively record his experience without distorting it to suit conventional morality and standard literary tastes. As he observed in "How Bigger Was Born," he began the novel "like a scientist in a laboratory," using his imagination to invent "test tube situations" (xxi) that would allow him to define a problem clearly and then rigorously study it.

More importantly, Wright was influenced by naturalism as a deterministic vision of life, one that claimed human behavior was shaped by massive environmental forces such as heredity, biological necessity, social conditioning, and economic pressure. These forces, taken singly or in combination, could trap people by minimizing consciousness and overwhelming free will. Such a pessimistic philosophy provided Wright with a compelling way of viewing his own experiences as an American black person conditioned by a hostile white environment. *Native Son* is therefore deeply preoccupied with the impact of environment on the individual, and in nearly every major scene the novel raises the question of whether people are simply products of environmental conditioning or whether they can ultimately use consciousness and free will to achieve a human victory over an environment intent on reducing them to the level of trapped animals. Like Dreiser's *Sister Carrie*, Wright's masterwork carefully details the ways in which a modern urban world can shape behavior by putting people under constant economic and social pressures that threaten to numb consciousness and erode human will. Like Zola's *La Bête Humaine*, Wright's novel is also a profound study of how people under the weight of heredity and biological compulsion can erupt in terrible acts of self-destructive violence. And like Farrell's *Studs Lonigan*, *Native Son* is a sharp criticism of a modern American society that attempts to impoverish the central character's life by clouding his mind with trivialized values and chaining his body to sterile routines.

Whether or not *Native Son* is fully naturalistic in style and vision is a question critics have vigorously debated for many years. Our reading of the novel will address this question and the closely related question of Bigger's heroism by probing various aspects of the book's form, especially setting, structure, characterization, point of view, and tone. This formal analysis demonstrates that Bigger Thomas is initially portrayed as a naturalistic victim caught in an environmental trap but eventually becomes a new kind of black hero when he develops the psychological resources necessary to understand and, in several important ways, master his environment. In other words, *Native Son* ultimately provides a vision of life that can be called existential because it affirms the possibility of humanly significant, indeed heroic, action after its central character has used his collisions with environment to create a human self centered in consciousness and free will.

Throughout this reading it is important to remember that form and content in *Native Son* are not separate entities but are organically fused with each other. *Native Son*'s triumph as a work of art lies in the fact that Wright was able not only to project the experience of American black people in all its raw brutality but also to *form* it into a rich, coherent, balanced vision of life. The novel is therefore much more than the "powerful" but artistically flawed piece of crude naturalism that many early reviewers and some later critics mistakenly saw. It is a masterwork because its formal artistry and its revolutionary new content are solidly integrated to produce a complex and resonant vision of modern American reality.

5

Setting

From the very outset of the novel Wright makes it clear in his depiction of setting that his central character is forced to inhabit a brutally deterministic environment, one at odds with his most fundamental human drives. The first word of the opening scene describes the harsh ringing of an alarm clock that shocks Bigger Thomas into an awakened state in much the same way as Pavlov's dogs were conditioned by the ringing bells that mechanically directed their reflex actions. As the lights are turned on, we become aware of an entire family packed into a "tiny" (8) one-room apartment that denies them space and privacy, reducing them to the status of cornered animals.

The grossly dehumanizing qualities of such an environment are further stressed when "a huge black rat" (9) is spotted in the room and Bigger is commanded by his terror-stricken mother to kill it. While his sister huddles in a "corner" (8), Bigger kills the rat, by first stunning it with a skillet and then crushing its head with a shoe. What makes this scene especially horrifying is the way Wright subtly associates the situation of the rat with the condition of the people forced to kill it. Just as Vera retreats into a corner to escape the rat, the rat itself is cornered by

Bigger. And as the rat "pulsed with fear" (9), so too do Mrs. Thomas and her children look upon the rat with "horror" (8). When Bigger eventually waves the rat's corpse at Vera, "enjoying his sister's fear" (11), he is using the display of bravado as a way of deflecting attention from his own considerable fear. The rat—described as running in a "narrow circle" (9) in a fruitless attempt to avoid death because it cannot escape through the baseboard hole, which Buddy has blocked— is very much like the Thomas family, who are likewise trapped in a squalid room that contains a door leading only into another trap, the ghetto.

The comparisons between the rat and Bigger are particularly revealing. While Bigger's face is set with "clenched teeth" (9) as he is pushed into "violent action" (8) to preserve himself and his family, the rat is likewise forced by circumstances to attack Bigger violently with its teeth, which are described as "two long yellow tusks" (10). Before the rat dies it emits a piercing shriek, "a long thin song of defiance" (9), and, in a similar way, Bigger is presented as "cursing hysterically" (10) while delivering his death blows to the rat. Perhaps subconsciously sensing the connection between himself and the cornered animal he stalks and kills, Bigger finally expresses "awed admiration" (10) for the rat, impressed by its size, strength, and defiance.

In "How Bigger Was Born" Wright claimed that he wanted the novel to read dramatically, like "a movie unfolding upon the screen" (xxxii). The opening scene of *Native Son* employs close-up shots to portray the personal lives of the Thomas family as warped by a grimly deterministic setting. In the scenes that immediately follow, Wright widens his camera angle, providing panoramic shots of the city in which his characters live. But as he moves from an oppressively small, one-room apartment to the larger world of Chicago's South Side, the environment remains the same, a trap that systematically strips people of human qualities. Everywhere Bigger goes he is reminded that he is a black man in a white world that denies him significant exercise of free will, and he is "maddened . . . that he did not have a wider course of action" (16). All the images of the city he perceives suggest this sense of restriction—the streetcars run on "steel tracks" (16), and everywhere he goes he sees walls. When he considers his limited options to his bleak life at home "his mind hit a blank wall" (16), and when he and Buddy talk they lean against "a red brick wall" (18). As Bigger looks up at an election poster of a white man running for district attorney, he is reminded that "IF YOU BREAK THE LAW, YOU CAN'T WIN" (16). When he looks up again and is inspired by the sight of a plane flying overhead, he is informed by Gus that only whites are given the opportunity to fly such planes literally or otherwise become upwardly mobile in American life. Indeed, Bigger again feels like the rat depicted in the novel's first scene. Just as the rat is safe only when it stays behind its baseboard hole but will starve if it remains there all the time, Bigger feels "like I'm on the outside of the world peeping through a knot-hole in the fence" (23). When he tries to break through that hole in order to "feed" himself on the opportunities of American life, he realizes that such opportunities do not exist for blacks. As he tells Gus, "They don't let us do anything" (22). He knows that black people, like the rat, are cornered, for they are forced to live in a teeming ghetto that denies them social, economic, and political possibilities, and Bigger thus sees this ghetto metaphorically as "one corner of the city" (23). Physically trapped by a racist society that treats blacks as animals, Bigger perceives his life as "like living in jail" (23) because his experiences both at home and in the larger world deny him basic forms of human action. Either way he turns, the setting reminds him of his hopeless situation. If he accommodates himself to the expectations of the dominant society, he will be condemned to live in a rat-infested apartment, and if he rebels, he will, as Buckley's campaign poster warns him, end up in jail or worse. The urban setting, in both its microcosmic and its macrocosmic forms, imprisons Bigger, bottling up his deepest human impulses and forcing him to live like an animal.

Wright's portrayal of the setting in the early parts of the novel is therefore classically naturalistic. He meticulously photographs reality in the ghetto to suggest that the physical details of Bigger's world reflect the powerful deterministic forces that deplete his consciousness and limit his field of action. For most of the remainder of the novel, however, Wright does not use photographic methods to depict Bigger's environment in a literal way; instead, he employs a wide range of surrealistic techniques to portray the city as a reflector of Bigger's psychological and emotional states. But the net effect is once again deterministic. Just as Wright, early in the novel, carefully photographs the outer setting to define the external forces conditioning Bigger's behavior, he then artfully distorts the outer appearance of the city to reflect the inner forces that press upon Bigger and control his actions. In other words, we see the setting as it is filtered through Bigger's highly pressured thoughts, emotions, and instincts.

Wright first uses this surrealistic technique in presenting Bigger's initial contacts with the Dalton family, for whom he must work as a chauffeur in order to earn enough money to provide his family with a subsistence level of existence. Because Bigger has lived in a rigidly segregated society that has given him only limited contacts with whites and because most of these contacts have been negative and at one point have actually resulted in the death of his father in a race riot, he views the world of the Daltons through a thick filter of fear, anxiety, and mistrust. When Wright first describes the Dalton home, he is therefore intent not on rendering the scene objectively but on pushing external reality through Bigger's pressurized mind. As a result, the Dalton's opulent home on Drexel Boulevard is strangely exaggerated, becoming a mindscape more than an objectively real place: "The houses he passed were huge; lights glowed softly in the windows. The streets were empty, save for an occasional car that zoomed past on swift rubber tires. This was a cold and distant world; a world of white secrets carefully guarded. . . . He came to Drexel Boulevard and began to look for 4605. When he came to it, he stopped and stood before a high, black picket fence, feeling constricted inside. All he felt in the movie was gone; only fear and emptiness filled him now." (45). Wright makes no attempt here to provide a fully detailed photographic like-ness of the house. He selects only those details which suggest Bigger's emotions of fear and emptiness and then shapes them into a blurry, dreamlike picture. Thus the streets are "empty" and the houses are "huge," strangely lighted, and filled with "white secrets," to make us feel the disorienting emotions Bigger experiences as he regards the scene. Bigger's emotional distance from such a strange, "cold" world is suggested by the "high black iron picket fence" that makes him feel not only trapped ("constricted") but also excluded. Again he feels he is on the outside of the world looking in.

As the pressures within Bigger gradually increase, producing more intense emotions and biological urges, the setting becomes progressively more distorted because everything he sees in the external world is filtered through these inward forces, which condition both his perception and his behavior. The sequence in which he rides with Jan and Mary through various part of South Side Chicago is a vivid example. Feeling desperately uneasy as he sits between these two white people in the car speeding through the night, he looks out the window and sees the lakefront as "a huge, flat sheet of gleaming water" (68) that is threatened by strong winds and darkened by storm clouds. Although Mary perceives the scene in lyrical terms, describing it as "beautiful" (68), for Bigger it is an ominous reflection of the troubled "waters" within him that are soon to be violently riled with his own uncontrollable emotional "storms." As he drives to Ernie's Chicken Shack, he looks at "tall, dark apartment buildings looming to either side of them" (70) and feels intimidated also by his own smallness, a feeling brought on by his being with rich whites whom he often sees as powerful forces in nature or omnipotent gods. When he enters Ernie's, he feels "ensnared in a tangle of deep shadows, shadows as black as the night that stretched above his head" (72). Again the details of the outward setting are used to reflect the dark forces inside Bigger. Caught in a tangle of "shadowy" emotions triggered by his bringing these strange white people into a restaurant frequented only by blacks, Bigger perceives the external setting as an extension of his own troubled feelings.

This mildly surrealistic treatment of setting intensifies after Bigger drinks heavily at Ernie's and later in the car. Although he consumes rum and beer to calm himself and steady his perceptions, the effect of his drinking is the exact reverse of what he intends. The more inebriated he becomes, the more his grip on external reality loosens, causing him to see the urban landsacpe as a nightmare. As he drives slowly through the winding roads of Washington Park, he gets the sense that "[h]e was not driving; he was simply sitting and floating along smoothly through darkness" (77–78). Eventually he loses nearly all contact with the setting as an objectively real place: "His sense of the city and the park fell away; he was floating in the car" (78). Such a literal drive through the "dark park" (77) is also a psychological journey through the winding corridors leading to Bigger's dark subconscious mind, where fear and hatred boil furiously, eventually exploding in terrible violence in Mary's bedroom.

When Bigger's emotions go beyond certain thresholds of intensity, the setting becomes a strangely gothic world reflecting those emotions. Returning to the Dalton home after driving Jan and Mary through Washington Park, Bigger is so inflamed with alcohol, sexual desire, and a deep-seated hostility toward whites that he sees the "dark and silent" (84) home as a kind of haunted house. Caught in the grip of "hysterical terror" (84) when Mrs. Dalton enters Mary's bedroom just as he is about to make love to her, Bigger has the feeling that he is "falling from a great height in a dream" (84), so detached is he from external circumstances as he withdraws into the murky world of his mind. Mrs. Dalton at this point becomes a "ghostlike" figure, a "white blur" (84), and Mary's room itself is bathed in a "hazy blue light" (85). After Mrs. Dalton leaves the room, Bigger becomes terrified that he has killed Mary and plunges even more deeply into nightmare: "The reality of the room fell from him; the vast city of white people that sprawled outside took its place" (86). But whether the setting takes the form of a strange room in a haunted house or that of "a vast city" of angry whites, the result is the same, since each is an image reflecting the deep fears overwhelming Bigger's conscious mind and forcing him into reflexive acts of violence sparked by the irrational forces within him.

In the remainder of the novel, images of the city get progressively more surrealistic as Bigger's mind is submitted to even greater pressures. When Bigger visits Bessie to calm his fears of being caught as Mary's killer, the city he walks through is given a Poe-esque quality.

Setting

Street lamps cast a ghastly "yellow sheen," and the lamps themselves are described as "round hazy balls of light frozen into motionlessness" (124). After Bigger and Bessie return from the Paris Grill, they pass through an urban environment strangely transformed by deep snow, strong winds, and eerie light. The "black, looming, empty apartment buildings" (140) intensify their fears, and the streets become "long paths through a dense jungle, lit here and there by torches" (140). Such brilliant effects, suggestive of a film noir or an expressionistic painting, bring the reader deeply inside the shadowy jungle of Bigger's subconscious mind.

Wright, who greatly admired Poe's fiction, at key points in the novel portrays Chicago in much the same way as Poe describes Paris in "The Murders of the Rue Morgue" or London in "The Man of the Crowd." Chicago becomes a sinister underworld reflective of man's darkest irrational nature when Bigger walks through the city to find a building to use as a drop-off point for the ransom he tries to extort from the Daltons. Walking through ghetto streets at night, Bigger sees "empty buildings with black windows like blind eyes" (163), reminding him of "blind" people like the Daltons and Buckley whom he fears will punish him. This setting also reveals Bigger's intense fear of death, for he sees such buildings as "skeletons with snow on their bones in the winter winds" (163). As Bigger proceeds through this grotesque environment, a city he feels is "tumbling down from rot" (163), the reader sees such an external world as quite like Poe's House of Usher, a place reflecting the psychic disintegration of a character gradually being consumed by fear and guilt.

When Bigger's experiences become even more turbulent and extreme, his environment becomes more violently surreal. While he and Bessie are involved in the extortion plot that causes them to undergo increasing levels of stress, their emotional "storm" is dramatized by the raging blizzard through which they struggle as they try to reach the abandoned building where they have planned to pick up the money. Likewise, when Bigger escapes from the police after they discover that he has probably killed Mary, the city into which he runs is aboil with violent natural forces that outwardly frustrate him and reveal the storm of emotions raging within him. He lowers his head against the "driving snow" and pushes on with "clenched fists" (208) through the icy, windy streets. The street lamps are coated with snow and resemble "frosted moons," while the falling snow forms a "gauze-like curtain" (208) that further confounds Bigger's vision. This surreal environment becomes even stranger when Bigger takes Bessie to the abandoned building in which he rapes and kills her. The windows of this building appear to him as the "eye-sockets of empty skulls" (216). Once again the external world falls away from Bigger—he feels that "the city did not exist" as he becomes entranced by the "black-dark and silent" (221) room, which, like Mary's bedroom, becomes a symbol of his dark subsconscious mind. As he resolves to kill Bessie, he listens to the wind's moaning "like an idiot in an icy black pit" (221).

After he kills Bessie and tries to escape, Bigger again experiences the city as "a strange labyrinth" (225). Furthermore, the record-breaking snowfall has clogged Chicago's roads and a citywide man-hunt has resulted in police searching all buses and autos. Physically "blocked," Bigger is also mentally and emotionally "trapped" (230). When the police catch him he is completely paralyzed, perched impotently above a water tower high atop a ghetto building, walled in by icy winds and frozen by cold jets of water that the police use to immobilize him.

Throughout *Native Son*, then, setting is consciously used to remind us of the powerful environmental forces both inside and outside Bigger that eventually make him helpless. The more he tries to assert free will in external acts of rebellion against his environment, the more this environment conspires to close in upon him, ultimately trying to trap him in precisely the same way he had earlier trapped the rat.

6

Structure

Impressive evidence of the formal artistry of *Native Son* is revealed not only in its conscious use of setting but also in its structure. Both in the way Wright carefully constructed the novel's plot and in the way he ingeniously crafted intricate patterns of imagery to reinforce the plot's central meanings, he was able to build a novel that was well equipped to dramatize his vision of life powerfully and coherently. In the beginning of the novel its networks of imagery and its narrative structure work together to define the massive environmental forces conditioning the central character. Gradually, however, an important reversal takes place as patterns of action and imagery reveal Bigger's growing awareness of how environment works. Although he is never able to master his outward environment by literally reshaping it to suit his needs, Bigger can gain control over himself and undergo significant inward growth, thus achieving a human dignity that the outward environment is intent on destroying.

The key to the novel's structure is contained in "How Bigger Was Born," in which Wright discusses the actual composition of his book. He reveals that he tried 20 or 30 times to write an appropriate opening scene and, failing to do this, plunged into the writing of the novel, starting with the pool hall scene and eventually producing a rough first draft. He then went back to writing the novel's opening scene, in search of one that would provide "the type of concrete event that would convey the motif of the entire scheme of the book, that would sound, in varied form, the note that was to be resounded throughout its length, that would introduce to the reader just what kind of organism Bigger's was and the environment that was bearing hourly upon it" (xxix). What Wright was searching for was an episode that would, like the first two pages of Joyce's *Portrait of the Artist as a Young Man,* telescope the entire novel, using images and action that would resonate in various forms throughout the book. Such a "motif" would "sound in various form the note that was to be resounded throughout its length" in much the same way as a musical composition might state its central theme in the beginning and then present a complex set of variations on that theme.

The narrative structure of *Native Son* can thus be seen as an elaborate sequence of scenes that are organized as a series of concentric circles, reverberating against one another to produce effects that become richer and more complex as the novel develops. The initial scene, which depicts the Thomas family as trapped by environmental forces threatening to reduce them to the status of animals, centers the novel, and all its major scenes radiate from this center in somewhat the same way as waves issue forth from the impact of a stone upon a body of water. But it is important to realize that as these scenes radiate from the initial scene they do not merely repeat its meaning. Rather, they offer *variations* on that first scene, producing more complex meanings as the central character grows, while his experiences bring him to larger frames of action that broaden his perspective and deepen his consciousness. As the scenes progress, Bigger develops as a human being.

The overall purpose of the novel, as Wright explained in 'How Bigger Was Born," is to explore "just what kind of organism Bigger was" and to probe the kind of "environment that was bearing hourly" upon him. Narrative structure, like setting, is used to explore the

problem central to all classic naturalistic novels, namely the relationship between the individual and the environment. The response given
to this problem in book 1 leads to a largely deterministic interpretation
of the novel. The three major scenes in book 1—Bigger's killing of the
rat, his near killing of Gus, and his accidental killing of Mary
Dalton—are all scenes of entrapment in which various forces inside
and outside the central character restrict his consciousness and limit
his free will, thereby forcing him into acts of reflexive violence that
become more serious as the scenes progress. Bigger really has no
choice but to kill the rat as his own fears and the frenzied promptings
of his family coerce him into action. As we have seen, Bigger and the
rat are presented as cornered animals that must lash out with instinctive acts of violence in an attempt to protect themselves. When Bigger
attacks Gus in the poolroom he is in essentially the same situation. His
intense fear of robbing a white-owned grocery store and his equally
intense fear of revealing his anxieties to his black cohorts result in his
striking out with a compensatory violence against Gus. Just as he had
earlier tormented his sister with the rat's corpse to hide his own fear,
Bigger now tortures Gus with a knife to cover up his own fear. And
just as the Thomas family was paralyzed with dread in the first scene,
now Gus is rendered motionless in this subsequent scene. In each scene
Bigger is described as a frenzied animal—cursing hysterically as he
crushes the rat's head in the opening episode and becoming "an animal
leaping" (40) at Gus in the subsequent scene. And in each scene Bigger's mode of attack is similar—he uses the sharp "gleaming" (40)
blade of his knife to terrify Gus just as the rat had attacked him with
its equally sharp "yellow fangs" (10).

Bigger also acts out the role of the cornered animal in Mary's
bedroom. Again he is "frozen with fear" (81), caught as he is between
his biological urge to make love to Mary and the social conditioning
that tells him he will pay a terrible price if he does so and is caught.
When Mrs. Dalton enters the room, he therefore feels seized by "a
hysterical terror" (84) and accidentally smothers Mary so that she
cannot make any sounds that would reveal his presence to her mother,
whom he sees as a symbol of white society.

The images used in these three scenes are carefully structured in elaborate patterns to accentuate the deterministic nature of Bigger's experiences. At the outset of each scene, particular noises trigger reflexive actions. Images of blindness and darkness reinforce the idea that Bigger is stripped of the consciousness necessary to bring these actions under control. And images of entrapment describe the net effect of such blind actions because these actions serve only to trap Bigger in a mounting pattern of violence that will eventually lead to his destruction. Finally, images of circularity reveal that Bigger's acts of violence are futile repetitions of one another, locking him in compulsive behavior that will ultimately destroy him.

These key scenes artfully use noise imagery to show how Bigger is often conditioned by his violent environment. Just as the alarm clock jolts Bigger into a dazed state of semiawareness and shock at the beginning of the novel, Gus's casual whistling of "The Merry-Go-Round Broke Down" sets off Bigger's anger as he enters the pool hall, an anger that releases Bigger's pent-up feelings of fear and results in his kicking Gus to the floor and threatening him with a knife. In a similar way, the creaking of the door of Mary's bedroom when her mother enters just as Bigger is ready to make love to Mary sends Bigger into a frenzy of violent behavior.

In each of these three scenes the characters' greatly reduced capacity for lucid consciousness is also dramatized by Wright's careful use of ocular imagery. In the novel's first scene Bigger is described as "rubbing his eyes" (7) to adjust his vision from total darkness to sudden brightness when the lights are switched on. Because the ensuing action happens so quickly, he has difficulty bringing his eyes into sharp focus and his killing of the rat comes more from the fuzzy promptings of instinct than clear deliberation. Bigger's vision is also defective in the pool room scene. As he flashes the knife before Gus's face, Bigger's expression is characterized by "the hard glint in his bloodshot eyes" (40). Gus, whose eyes have earlier been described as "dead-black with hate" (39), is so terrified by Bigger that his "lips quivered and tears streamed down his face" (41). Pushed to emotional extremities, his vision blurs. Ocular images are structured in a particularly elaborate way when Bigger kills Mary, again to suggest that the characters are blinded by environmental conditioning and emotional intensity. When Bigger brings Mary into the bedroom, her eyes are described as "closed" (80) and "blank" (83) because her vision has been nearly incapacitated by drinking too much rum. When she later uses her eyes to look at Bigger to arouse him sexually, her eyes gaze at him "feverishly from dark sockets" (81). Mary's "dark sockets" suggest that she is blind to the powerful emotional forces she is releasing in Bigger, societally formed anxieties and hatreds that are more likely to move him toward violence than love. Bigger's eyes are also presented as badly out of focus and thus unable to perceive reality in any clear way. Disoriented by the room's "hazy blue light" (85), he sees Mrs. Dalton as "a white blur" that "filled his eyes and gripped his body" (84). She becomes a kind of ghost, inducing in him a frenzy that blinds him to the fact that she is a frail woman whom he could easily evade by merely slipping under the bed.

The powerful effect of environment is further stressed in these scenes with carefully wrought images of entrapment, particularly in the form of walls and circularity. Such entrapment offers two equally destructive options: paralysis or violence. The rat in the opening scene is thrown up against the wall of the Thomas's claustrophobic apartment, and when it tries to fight back it is killed. The "narrow circle" (9) in which the rat runs before being killed is a revealing symbol of its trapped condition. In the poolroom scene the characters' lives are presented as enervating routines that occasionally erupt in violence. The poolroom itself is a confining place where Bigger and his friends waste much of their time in repetitious loafing. When Bigger attacks Gus he treats him in a way quite similar to the way he had earlier treated the rat, hurling Gus to the floor and then threatening him with violence to the head. More importantly, Bigger himself is seen as physically and emotionally cornered. Right before he attacks Gus, he "staggers back against the wall" (40), a sign that his violence comes from his own pent-up mind, earlier described as having walls that protect Bigger from his fears. As he threatens Gus with the knife by waving it in front of Gus's shirt "as though cutting a circle" (41), Bigger becomes further ensnared by his instinct for violence, which traps him in a circle of compulsion.

Images of walls and circularity are also used with telling effect in the scenes culminating with Mary's death and dismemberment. This sequence, which begins with Bigger "circling [Mary's] waist" (82) as he carries her upstairs to her bedroom and ends with his observing the "widening circles of pink on the newspapers" (91) as he examines her severed head, shows Bigger encircled with emotions he can neither understand nor control. He is therefore trapped throughout the scene. Entering Mary's dark bedroom, he "felt along the wall" (83) in a vain attempt to find a light. When Mrs. Dalton enters the room, he is "afraid to move" (84), and when she moves forward toward Mary's bed, he noiselessly steps to the opposite side of the room, "his muscles so taut they ached" (85). The final effect of this scene, of course, is to doom Bigger, because his violence toward a white woman will inevitably result in his own incarceration and death.

Book 2, entitled "Flight," is apparently structured in the same way as book 1, for it too is organized by three major scenes of entrapment laced with patterns of deterministic imagery. Throughout book 2, however, Wright suggests that there is a way out of the naturalistic trap for Bigger if he can overcome his blindness and see his environment truly and then imagine alternatives to it. Although the three major scenes—Bigger's murder of Bessie, his escape from the authorities, and his capture by the police—portray Bigger as repeating patterns of behavior brought on by environmental conditioning, they also provide important evidence that he is gaining the ability to break the circle of necessity that has dominated him for so long. He is thus able to make the first steps toward the new life he will more fully achieve in book 3.

Bigger's murder of Bessie, on the surface, seems to be only a grim reenactment of his earlier killings of the rat and Mary Dalton. Once more he attacks by going for the head, this time using a brick to crush Bessie's skull. Here again Bigger is motivated by fears brought on by environmental conditioning. Because he was afraid to act alone in extorting money from the Daltons, he involved Bessie in his plans, and now that he is afraid Bessie will disclose information to the police that will result in his capture, he feels "he would have to kill her. It was his life against hers" (222). Imagery from the earlier scenes also crowd this scene, suggesting that it is part of a circle of repetition of mounting violence going back to the very first pages of the novel. When Bigger and Bessie enter the abandoned building where he rapes and kills her, they hear "the scurrying of quick, dry feet" (217), rats that inspire in Bessie the same urge to scream that earlier overcame Bigger's mother and sister. The "black darkness" (217) of the room recalls Mary's darkened bedroom. And as Bigger resolves to kill Bessie, he enters the same trancelike state that overcame him as he suffocated Mary. As his "heart beat wildly," the "reality of it all slipped from him" (222). Before he kills Bessie, Bigger consciously makes connections between what he is currently experiencing and prior events, as he is nearly overcome by "[a] sense of the white blur hovering near, of Mary burning, of the law tracking him down" (223). Images of circularity are also used to stress that Bigger is compulsively repeating violent episodes from his past life. He waves the flashlight's beam in a circular pattern over Bessie's face as he earlier threatened Gus by tracing with his knife a circular pattern over Gus's chest. The whiskey he consumes makes his head "whirl" (217) as the rum he earlier drank helped send his head spinning in Mary's bedroom. When he rapes Bessie he feels overwhelmed by the same erotic desires he felt for Mary, sensing that he is "on some vast turning wheel that made him want to turn faster and faster" (219).

But there are significant differences to be drawn between the Bigger who kills Bessie and the Bigger who earlier killed the rat, intimidated Gus, and accidentally suffocated Mary. The Bigger Thomas portrayed in this scene placed approximately midway through the novel is very much more *conscious* of his actions and, although this quality in one way makes his actions more reprehensible, in another way it shows a kind of growth in his personality. Whereas Bigger is prompted by his family to kill the rat, here he acts alone. Whereas his treatment of Gus and Mary stemmed from frenzied passions that blurred his vision and reduced his responsibility for his actions, in this scene he eventually acts from lucid, carefully deliberated motives. Certainly the most chilling aspect of Bigger's murder of Bessie is that he twice turns on the light before attacking her, consciously grips the brick with his hand, gets a full view of her sleeping face, turns off the light again so as not to awaken her, and then coldly kills her by knocking her unconscious and throwing her into an air shaft, where she eventually freezes. Whereas Bigger's earlier violence was instinctive, this brutal killing is ultimately a conscious act, his successful attempt "to impose his will over his body" (222). And whereas his earlier acts of violence stemmed from situations in which Bigger "closed his eyes and struck out blindly" (225), this terrible act is clearly envisioned, highly calculated.

Wright surely views Bigger with horror here and rejects his character's romanticizing of his murder of Bessie, just as he earlier undercut with irony Bigger's gloating over his killing of Mary. Wright stresses that Bigger's killing of Mary was not a conversion experience providing him with a "new life" (101) but simply brought to a culmination the pathological tendencies of Bigger's old life. So too does Wright reject Bigger's claim that in killing Bessie he was "living truly and deeply" and that such an act was one of "the most meaningful acts that had ever happened to him" (225). Nevertheless, Wright does validate Bigger's impression that "never had his will been so free as in this day of fear and murder and flight" (225). Unlike Bigger's other acts of violence in the novel, his murder of Bessie involves genuine consciousness and free will. Although environmental pressures certainly play a significant role in the scene, they do not wholly drive the action. Wright clearly does not glorify the way Bigger exercises his free will here, but he does present Bigger's murder of Bessie as a pivotal scene, because it is Bigger's fullest expression of free will up to this point in the novel and because it leads to other decisive acts of will. Even though several of Wright's friends, after reading the manuscript, were so repulsed by the scene that they urged him to delete it from the book, Wright emphasized the scene's importance by stubbornly insisting that the scene remain in the book as he wrote it.

As Bigger escapes from the police after killing Bessie, his consciousness deepens and he is able to assert his free will in several ways, even in the face of an environment growing ever more hostile. Although he is not able to overcome this environment by either escaping from or transforming it, he can acquire a lucid view of the world around him for the first time in his life and thus can begin to gain psychological distance from and emotional control over that world. In this way he takes crucial steps toward selfhood, planting seeds that eventually flower in book 3. While trying to find his way through the labyrinthine streets of Chicago's South Side, for example, he obtains a new perspective on his life as a black American when he climbs to the top of a tenement building and observes a black family living in a one-room apartment similar to the one he and his family rent. When he sees three black children in a bed watching their parents copulating, Bigger thinks, "Five of 'em sleeping in one room and here's a great big empty building with just me in it" (231). Descending from the roof to secure food and warmth, he walks through the streets, again thinking of the social system restricting blacks to impoverished ghettos: "They keep us bottled up here like wild animals" (233). Soon after, he sees "a big black rat" (231) leaping through the snow in search of a hole to provide it protection from the cold. In contrast to the first scene, in which Bigger's frenzied emotions canceled out his conscious thoughts, reducing him to the level of an animal, Bigger here retains a human identity by continuing to think clearly. He carefully looks for a Negro bakery to buy bread, knowing full well that a white proprietor might recognize and report him. Failing to find a black-owned bakery because the only black businesses in the ghetto are funeral parlors, he thinks again about how the social system oppresses blacks: "They trick us every breath we draw. . . . They gouge our eyes out" (234). Shortly afterward, he has another moment of awareness when he goes to an abandoned building and observes from a window a religious service in a black church. Although the church is "dim-lit" (237), Bigger's mind is illuminated by another significant insight: Conventional religion is a way in which black people are blinded by the system. As he listens to the congregation singing "Steal way, steal away to Jesus," he consciously rejects this kind of "surrender, rejection" (237). Even though he is in certain ways attracted to the music because it provides him with a systematic vision of life that satisfies "his deep yearning for a sense of wholeness" (238), he honestly faces up to the fact that such a vision is a set of illusions that encourage blacks to endure passively the injustices of the real world by offering them happiness in a vaguely imagined afterlife.

Rather than "steal away" to a comforting but false religion that would only stunt the growth of his fast-developing consciousness, Bigger for the remainder of book 2 continues to widen and deepen his view of things. He is finally captured in a scene filled with images of noise, confinement, and circularity, images reminiscent of the novel's first scene. But Bigger by this point has grown to the extent that this episode generates very different meanings. He no longer is a trapped rat driven by fear but has attained the sort of lucid consciousness that enables him to think and act freely. Even though the scene begins with a wild cacophony of "horns, sirens, screams" (241) that suggests the alarm clock of the first scene, and even though the spotlights "circle slowly" (241) in the dark to enclose Bigger behind "a shifting wall of light" (241–42), he can now face such a naturalistic trap with consciousness, will, and courage. Bigger indeed realizes that his current situation is the culmination of a long series of events: "He was in the midst of it now; this was what he was running from ever since Mrs. Dalton had come into the room and charged him with such fear" (242). But he does not run from his plight now, steadied by "an almost mystic feeling that if he were ever cornered something in him would prompt him to act the right way" (242). He resolves to defy his pursuers in a final showdown and in the process begins to overcome the fears that have trapped him for most of his life. As he is physically apprehended by the policemen who are emissaries from an "ocean of boiling hate" (249), he psychologically frees himself from the terror that environment has always imposed upon him and that, ironically, is currently driving the police:

> He knew they were afraid, and yet he knew it would soon be over, one way or the other: they would either capture or kill him. He was surprised he was not afraid. Under it all some part of his mind was

beginning to stand aside; he was going behind his curtain, his wall, looking out with sullen stares of contempt. He was outside of himself now, looking on; he lay under a winter sky lit with tall gleams of whirling light, hearing thirsty screams and hungry shouts. He clutched his gun, defiant, unafraid. (250–51)

Now it is the social world outside Bigger that behaves like animals driven by "thirsty screams" and "hungry shouts." Bigger, on the other hand, is detached from such a world of instinctive violence. Because "some part of his mind was beginning to stand aside" from the world of hate and fear encircling him, he can direct his thoughts freely. Retreating to an inward world he is just beginning to become consciously aware of, he can become anchored in a new sense of self. The "walls" he goes behind now are very different from the mental walls and "curtains" he retreated behind at the end of the first scene, for these new walls psychologically distance him from fear instead of repressing fear. Whereas the walls inside Bigger's mind were earlier described as blocking his vision, these new walls allow him to look out at a deterministic environment with "sullen stares of contempt," thus giving him necessary critical awareness of an external world intent on blinding him. As a result, he can be "defiant" and "unafraid" in a *public* way for the first time in his life, not feeling the need either to subvert secretly or to cower from the white world he no longer fears. Bigger's captors try to intimidate him just as he had earlier intimidated Vera and Gus, but they succeed only in strengthening his defiance. Indeed, Bigger "laughs" (252) as the police capture him, savoring the awareness that "they are afraid" (252), trapped as they are in societally induced ignorance and hatred. The final scene of book 2 therefore bristles with provocative ironies, since Bigger's developing consciousness frees him from the psychological burdens of environment precisely at the point where his body is imprisoned by agents of that environment. He emerges from the scene not as a trapped rat but as someone like Camus's Sisyphus, outwardly chained to an absurd task but inwardly liberated by his awareness that he is psychologically stronger than the angry gods who punish him.

This crucial moment of awareness Bigger achieves at the end of book 2 becomes the basis for his dramatic human growth in book 3. The final section of the novel, like the previous two books, pivots on these crucial scenes, each of which takes the form of a conversation. The conversations Bigger has with a variety of people as they visit his cell early in book 3, the dialogue he has with Max in the visiting room, and his final talk with Max at the end of the novel—all have the same effect, that of enriching Bigger's inward life so that he can achieve human selfhood despite a deterministic environment. These three scenes, then, allow Bigger ultimately to break the circle of necessity of his prior life and to achieve a new life grounded in existential freedom.

At the beginning of book 3, Bigger is still struggling between two conceptions of himself. Part of him is still victimized by environment, and this self is paralyzed not only by his prison setting but also by his "deep psychological reaction not to react to anything" (255). This Bigger Thomas is simply numbed by his experiences, refuses to eat or drink, and looks blankly at the floor, "his eyes like two still pools of black ink on his flaccid face" (255). While this naturalistic self has been defeated by environment and waits for death, an existential self begins to emerge, one centered in "the conviction that there was some way out" (256) of his trap, some "new mode of life" based upon a "new hope" (256). It is this second self that consciously rejects the fear and hatred that has blinded him for most of his life: "Toward no one in the world did he feel any fear now, for he knew that fear was useless; and toward no one in the world did he feel any hate now, for he knew that hate would not help him" (254).

The scene early in book 3 where Bigger sits in his cell and talks with a great many people is a vivid example of how these two selves collide inside Bigger. Certainly the "old" Bigger who killed Mary is still very much in evidence here. This Bigger envisions life nihilistically, as a "vast black silent void" (263), and fatalistically sees his life as a circle of meaningless repetition he is powerless to control, one who feels he is pinned "on a vast blind wheel turned by stray gusts of wind" (267). This is the same Bigger who is so trapped by negative emotions that he feels a powerful desire to "blot . . . from sight" (275) his family and friends when they express concern for him. But another, very different Bigger Thomas also struggles to assert himself in this scene: the man who can be so moved by Jan's kindness that he can regard Jan as "someone who had performed an operation on his eyes" (268), one whose example allows Bigger to begin to overcome the blindness that has inhibited his growth. Able to see the world in a new and humane way, Bigger is therefore able to experience a range of positive emotions he has earlier been afraid to acknowledge. Jan's words enable Bigger "for the first time in his life" to perceive "a white man as a human being" (268). Bigger is also able to express for the first time in the novel a love for his mother, embracing her and expressing sorrow for the difficulties he has caused her. Such new feelings allow him to overcome the extreme isolation he has suffered in nearly all the novel's episodes, forming a much-needed bond of kinship between him and the people around him: "He had lived and acted on the assumption that he was alone, and now he saw that he had not been. What he had done made others suffer. No matter how much he would long for them to forget him, they would not be able to. His family was a part of him, not only in blood, but in spirit" (277).

If Bigger is able to draw humanly close to those caring about him, he is also able to develop a healthy and aggressive sense of rebellion against those like Buckley who are interested in humiliating and punishing him. Looking at the enraged mob in the streets below his cell window, he resolves never to accept the dehumanizing labels they apply to him: "The atmosphere of the crowd told him that they were going to use his death as a bloody symbol of fear to wave before the eyes of that black world. As he felt it, rebellion rose in him. He had sunk to the lowest point this side of death, but when he felt his life again threatened in a way that meant he was to go down the dark road a helpless spectacle of sport for others, he sprang back into action, alive, contending" (257). Just as Bigger's new capacity for love enlivens him and humanizes him by bonding him with others who see him in human terms, his sense of rebellion makes him "spring back into action alive and contending" because it gives him an alternative to accepting passively the brutal images of himself offered by a pathological environment. Consciously resolving not to be a "bloody symbol of fear," Bigger elects to be a human being. He can therefore pursue his own road to "a sure and quiet knowledge" (236), rather than go down the "road" prepared for him by the white system that wants to reduce him to becoming "a helpless spectacle of sport for others."

In "How Bigger Was Born" Wright defended this scene in Bigger's cell by stressing that he wanted it to "elicit a certain emotional response from Bigger" even though Wright had to violate "surface reality or plausibility" (xxxi) by cramming so many people into Bigger's cell at one time. By thus confronting Bigger with nearly every important character with whom he has interreacted in the novel, Wright forces Bigger to review his entire life and to discover that he has two possibilities. If he continues to be the "old" Bigger trapped in naturalistic circumstances, he will end up by dying a meaningless death that concludes an equally meaningless life. But he can choose to become a new man, one who can learn from his experiences and work toward the achievement of a human self.

The next major scene, which takes place roughly halfway through book 3, shows Bigger moving strongly in that direction. As he meets with Max in the visitor's room to prepare his case, Bigger finds "that he wanted someone near him" (319) for the first time since his capture. He has been sobered by his previous conversations with the man occupying the cell next to him, a person driven mad by the racial injustices of American society. Bigger therefore seeks human companionship in order to balance himself and thus keep him from being sucked into the "hot whirlpool" of madness that has destroyed his fellow prisoner. In the conversation that follows, Bigger fully communicates with another human being for perhaps the first time in his life, intimately sharing emotions and thoughts that he has repressed in every other major scene in the novel. Whereas Bigger's distance from people has earlier been signaled by his failure to establish eye contact, he is now described as "looking straight into Max's eyes" (320). His earlier inability to trust people like Jan and Mary is also reversed, as the narrator makes clear that Bigger now "trusted Max" (321). As a result, Bigger is able to emerge from the "walls" and "curtains" he has previously hidden behind, telling Max things he has never communicated to anyone and was even afraid to acknowledge to himself. He makes the stark disclosure "I don't reckon I was ever in love with nobody" (326) and describes his killing of Mary and Bessie as rooted in the fear and hatred that have rushed in to fill the vacuum created by this absence of love. He even reveals to Max his darkest secret, the intense feeling of freedom he experienced after killing both women: "For a little while I was free. I was doing something" (328). Max responds to Bigger's remarks with understanding and compassion and furthermore helps Bigger to feel kinship with other oppressed people, for it is Max who expands Bigger's view of American social reality by reminding him that the system oppresses Jews, Communists, and other minorities as well as blacks. This is an important step in Bigger overcoming the terrible isolation that has inhibited his human development.

Because he has "spoken to Max as he had never spoke to anyone in his life," Bigger feels "a recognition of his life, of his feelings, of his person that he had never encountered before " (323). Strengthened by this altogether new sense of self-worth, he attains an important sense of psychological poise, "balanced on a hairline" (333), which enables him finally to mediate between the turbulent violence and numbing apathy described earlier as the two "rhythms of his life" (31). He can now center his life around "a thin, hard core of consciousness" (333) that helps him transcend his earlier blindness and isolation and then perceive "vague relationships between himself and other people" that he has "never dreamed of" (334). Put another way, he feels "poised on the verge of action and commitment" (319) leading to a significant human growth. But Bigger's growth midway through book 3 is extremely precarious and can easily be canceled out by the destructive emotions that have dominated his previous life. At the end of the scene, he thus begins vaguely to distrust Max's motives in helping him and this distrust dissolves some of the psychological poise he has just achieved, trapping him once again in blindness: "And what motive could Max have in helping? Why would Max risk that white tide of hate to help him? . . . A strong counter-emotion waxed in him, urging him, warning him to leave this newly seen and newly felt thing alone, that it would lead him to another blind alley, to deeper hate and shame" (334).

Bigger's consciousness midway through book 3 is too "thin" and "hard." It is therefore vulnerable to the destructive emotions of "hate and shame" that can erode consciousness and trap Bigger in the "blind alleys" he has always known. By the end of the novel, however, Bigger's consciousness has deepened and become tougher, more resilient, so that he can sustain his human impulses in a fuller way. The fears that threaten to unbalance him have been overcome by his achievement of "self-control" (385), enabling him to achieve a mature sense of himself and his world. Although some critics have interpreted the novel's final scene as generating negative meanings, beginning as it does with Bigger feeling numbed by the news of his death sentence and ending with him facing his death alone, a closer reading of the scene reveals strikingly affirmative meanings. In this scene Bigger tells his story more fully than ever before and thus opens his eyes to the real significance of his life, even though Max provides a disappointing audience because his own emotional shortcomings blind him to the rich human meanings contained in Bigger's story. Although Bigger wants to "force upon Max the reality of his living" (386), Max's background makes it impossible for him to assimilate what Bigger's story is saying. But the essential point of the scene is clearly made—in the act of telling his story, Bigger discovers a new sense of himself and thus finally achieves the human selfhood his environment tries to destroy.

Yet Bigger experiences this sense of self alone, as Camus's Meurseault also experienced selfhood alone in a jail cell. While Max and Bigger talk, they are portrayed as inhabiting different universes. Indeed, the narrator at one point remarks that "Max was on a different planet" (386) as Bigger attempts to engage him in dialogue. The imagery of the scene strongly suggests that Max is caught in a deterministic universe, blinded as he is by a simplistic understanding of Marxist theory that blurs his vision of Bigger as an individual and also leads him to envision history fatalistically, as a "wheel of blood" (362). While Bigger's consciousness expands as he reaches down to the deep feelings generated by his personal experiences, Max backs away from him and tries to retreat behind walls of cliché and abstraction that depersonalize the conversation and enable him to evade the profound implications of what Bigger is saying. When Bigger thanks Max for treating him as a human being, Max replies with a barrage of commonplaces, including "You're human, Bigger" (387), and "Men die alone, Bigger" (388). When Bigger makes an important but disturbing connection between himself and the people intent on executing him, suggesting that society will kill him because it is blinded by the same fears that provoked him to kill Bessie and Mary, Max diverts his attention by leading him to the window and giving him an uplifting talk about "the belief of men" (389) holding society together.

Fortunately, Wright calculates the scene so that the reader can see the human being whom Max has become blind to, realizing that although Max has become trapped by fear and abstraction, Bigger is liberated by distilling from his personal experience new thoughts grounded in his deepest feelings. When Bigger tells Max, "What I killed for I *am*!" (391–92), the reader is not blinded by the fear and misunderstanding that overcomes Max, because it is clear that Bigger is not romanticizing reflexive violence. Bigger does not claim that the violence itself was good; in fact, he has repented of such violence by realizing in guilt and horror how it has hurt many innocent people. But Bigger does stress that what he killed *for* must have been good because he killed to attain a sense of freedom and autonomy systematically denied him by his environment. Elated by the profound feelings of freedom and independence that his violence has generated and not by the killings themselves, Bigger now realizes that there are other, more humane ways to be free.

To stress Bigger's human growth, Wright dramatically reverses the meanings of key images used at the outset of the novel. Whereas Bigger's eyes are out of focus for much of the opening scene and he refuses to establish eye contact with people, here he looks directly at Max, whom he sees as "white, solid, real" (384). Whereas the harsh noise of the alarm clock in the first scene "galvanized" Bigger into "violent action" (8) in much the same way as Pavlov's dogs were stimulated by ringing bells, the harsh clanging of his cell door described in the novel's final sentence produces in Bigger no outward action at all but a richly ironic awareness that although he is physically trapped and about to meet his death, he is in fact freer and more alive than the novel's many blind people who continue to live their lives as automatons driven by a mechanistic environment. Bigger's "faint, wry, bitter smile" (392), however, does not make him a hardened cynic like Buckley, who is incapable of sympathizing with or understanding other people. Bigger's smile is not only "bitter," suggesting his anger over human injustice, but also "faint" and "wry," suggesting a kind of objective awareness of human limitation. Bigger's face therefore reflects the emotional complexity missing in the face described early in the novel, a face whose "clenched teeth" (8) suggested an animal consciousness similar to the rat he kills. Bigger's final words are therefore an attempt to reconcile himself with people whom he had earlier hurt—he reassures Max that he is "all right" and asks Max to "tell Ma I was all right" (392) and also wants to be remembered to Jan. Whereas Bigger was portrayed at the outset of the novel as thinking that "the moment he allowed what his life meant to enter fully into his consciousness, he would kill either himself or someone else" (14), he now has a radically different notion of what his life means and this awareness leads him to a respect for himself and a concern for others. The mental "wall" (14) that had blunted his feelings and masked him with a "tough" (14) exterior has been dismantled, and as a result, Bigger emerges from the novel very different from the cornered animal he was in the opening scene.

Native Son, then, is structured in such a way as to tell a story of human growth. While each of the novel's major scenes consciously echo one another, these scenes do not merely repeat themselves but resonate to produce variations that enrich, complicate, and finally transform the meanings established in the early scenes. What begins as a classically naturalistic novel depicting a small central character caught in massive environmental forces he can neither understand nor control finally becomes an existential novel focusing on the character's achieving an understanding of and a psychological control over that environment. The narrative patterns of book 1 consist of powerfully dramatized outer actions that trap the character in a circle of iron necessity. But this external narrative gradually gives way to an inward narrative emerging in book 2 and culminating in book 3, consisting mainly of a series of conversations in which an outwardly immobilized central character ultimately undergoes a journey to the self that awakens him to a world very different from the brutal environment that stuns and conditions him in the novel's opening scene. Central to Bigger's transformation is his realization that "[t]he impulsion to try to tell [his story] was as deep as had been the urge to kill" (386). Book 1, which is grounded in Bigger's accidental killing of Mary, book 2, which is centered in his conscious murder of Bessie, point Bigger inevitably down the road to the "gallows" (13) his mother predicts for him at the conclusion of the opening episode. But book 3 in which Bigger is transformed when his compulsion to kill has been displaced by an equally potent but humanizing drive to understand himself and others by honestly telling his story, allows Bigger to travel a different road, one leading to existential selfhood. This achievement of selfhood certainly does not allow Bigger simply to transcend the force of environment; after all, he is still in jail and will soon be executed by the state. But it does allow him to discover important human resources deeply within himself, a discovery that finally enables him to move from the status of a naturalistic victim to that of an existential hero.

7

Characterization

As a study of setting and structure clearly reveals, Wright conceived of Bigger Thomas in very complex terms. He emphasized this factor in "How Bigger Was Born" when he observed:

> Bigger, as I saw him, was a snarl of many realities; he had in him many levels of life.
>
> First, there was his personal and private life, that intimate existence that is so difficult to snare and nail down in fiction, that elusive core of being, that individual data of consciousness which in every man and woman is like that in no other. I had to deal with Bigger's dreams, his fleeting, momentary sensations, his yearnings, visions, his deep emotional responses.
>
> Then I was confronted with that part of him that was dual in aspect, wavering, that part of him which is so much a part of *all* Negroes and *all* whites. . . . He was an American because he was a native son but he was also a Negro nationalist in a vague sense because he was not allowed to live as an American (xxiii–xxiv).

Throughout the novel Bigger's humanity is therefore defined in both universal and highly particularized ways. He surely is a representative man, one who represents "all Negroes" and "all whites" because he enacts on a symbolic level the condition of modern man alienated from a mechanistic environment. But he is also a richly imagined individual whose consciousness forms a "core of being" that is unique, "like that in no other."

Unfortunately, the people who surround Bigger fail to see him adequately on either level. Most are altogether blind to the "personal and private life" that forms the basis for his individuality, and these people also distort their view of him with stereotypes rooted in their own emotional needs. Thus Mr. Dalton perceives him as a "boy" (143) he can help so as to relieve his own guilt over being a slumlord. Max sees Bigger as part of a social "problem" (301) he can understand only within the limits of the political ideology he needs to believe in. Mary envisions Bigger as a black stud, the forbidden fruit she can consume in order to rebel against a social system that has given her privileges but left her with a gnawing sense of guilt and boredom. Many characters make Bigger into a symbol but not the "meaningful and prophetic symbol" (xlv) Wright described in "How Bigger Was Born." Instead of envisioning Bigger as a modern everyman who is victimized by the depersonalized social environment that threatens the humanity of all people, they see him as a dark embodiment of otherness that provokes their fear and hostility. Thus Buckley characterizes Bigger as a "black mad dog" (374) and an "infernal monster" (376) who threatens to destroy civilization. The newspapers label Bigger an "ape" (260), and the white mob congregated outside Bigger's jail cell perceive him as "a figment of the black world which they feared" (257).

As we have seen, many critics also have the same difficulty in viewing Bigger as the fully imagined, three-dimensional character Wright developed. For example, James Baldwin and Ralph Ellison described Bigger as a depraved monster, so shocked by his extremely violent behavior that they failed to realize two important points: (1) Bigger's sometimes brutal behavior is triggered by a pathological social environment that pushes him beyond his powers of control and understanding and (2) even while engaged in outward behavior that may be described as monstrous, Bigger is always portrayed in complexly human terms by Wright, who goes to great lengths never to let us forget Bigger's very human inward life.

In short, Wright always makes us aware that "there were two Biggers" (236–37), an outward person conditioned by a brutally deterministic environment and another, inward person who struggles against and eventually gains some degree of autonomy over that environment. Like Bigger himself, who in the early part of book 3 feels that "the actual killing of Mary and Bessie was not what concerned him most" and who tries desperately "to know what had driven him to it" (286), Wright is more interested in probing the humane interior life of his central character than sensationalistically detailing the gothic horrors of his outward actions. Wright always depicts Bigger as "divided and pulled against himself" (27), a person struggling against the deterministic forces that are at odds with his basic human drives.

That Bigger is not a pathological monster but a richly imagined person is stressed in an early scene in which he is able for a few brief moments to relax and operate independently from the intense pressures of his environment. Hanging out on the city streets with Gus, Bigger demonstrates that he is not really the "tough" guy most people see but has a "soft," human side to his character, a side that aspires to a better life and a more fully realized self. Although one part of Bigger resents Gus and later almost kills him in a poolroom fight, another part of Bigger responds to Gus here in a personal, even affectionate way. Indeed, Bigger shares with his friend his most deeply felt longing, a desire not only to be a pilot but also to "fly" (14) beyond the harsh restrictions ruling his life. When Gus reminds him of the ways in which white society will frustrate these hopes, Bigger does not lash out with reflexive hatred but instead jokes about the situation, transforming his pain and resentment into a complexly ironic awareness that the two of them enjoy.

Bigger therefore has a human self that can use consciousness to mitigate the effects of his severely restrictive environment. This part of Bigger possesses all the normal human drives of a 20-year-old American male responding to what he perceives are the opportunities of American life. Leaning against a "brick wall" (13)—an obvious reminder of an environment intent on depriving him of these opportunities—he nevertheless can feel an understandable urge to transcend his narrow existence and become part of a fluid world of movement and possibility:

> Bigger took out his pack and gave Gus a cigarette; he lit his and held the match for Gus. They leaned their backs against the red brick wall of a building, smoking, their cigarettes slanting white across their black chins. To the east Bigger saw the sun burning a dappling yellow. In the sky above him a few white clouds drifted. He puffed silently, relaxed, his mind pleasantly vacant of purpose. Every slight movement in the street evoked a casual curiosity in him. Automatically, his eyes followed each car as it whirred over the smooth black asphalt. A woman came by and he watched the gentle sway of her body until she disappeared into a doorway. He sighed, scratched his chin and mumbled, "Kinda warm today." (13).

This is the Bigger Thomas whom most critics fail to see because his actions violate their standard view of him as a stereotyped "bad nigger" or victim of society. Despite the fact that Bigger will later kill two women after his normal drives toward love have been twisted by environment, here he takes an altogether normal pleasure in watching the "gentle sway" of a woman's body as she enters a building. And whereas the novel's key scenes of violence are acted out at night during powerful snowstorms that reflect his turbulent, uncontrolled emotions, Bigger here relaxes and enjoys the "sun burning dazzling yellow" and the white clouds floating in a clear, bright sky. Rigidly trapped in confining rooms throughout the novel, Bigger at this point is given a rare opportunity to become a part of the natural, fluid world that evokes his "casual curiosity." The fast-moving cars, the drifting clouds, the gracefully walking woman, and the high-flying plane touch Bigger at the core of his being, revealing a person who has all the usual American instincts for a life of change and possibility.

As environmental pressures later force Bigger into acts of terrible violence, Wright also makes us keenly aware of Bigger's inward, human self by skillfully probing the images that flit through the deepest levels of Bigger's subconscious mind, even as he performs these grisly acts. In the scenes following Mary's death, wherein Bigger amorally gloats over his killing of Mary, Wright makes us fully aware of Bigger's very moral inward nature by describing images arising from the conscience he is trying to suppress. One such image is the picture of Mary's severed head, an image that repeatedly torments Bigger. When he gets out of bed the morning after Mary's death, he is shaken when his subconscious mind generates "an image of Mary's head lying on the wet newspapers" (96). Riding a streetcar to the Dalton house a short while later, he consciously rejects any guilt over killing Mary— "He did not feel sorry for Mary; she was not real to him, not a human being" (108)—and he actually feels "justified" (108) in killing her. But on a deeper level of his mind he does respond to Mary as a person and feels profoundly troubled about killing her, for he cannot get "that lingering image of Mary's head . . . from before his eyes" (108). When Bigger arrives at the Dalton house this image becomes even more vivid and Bigger's moral reaction becomes even more explicit. He is compulsively drawn to the furnace in the basement, and when he opens the furnace door, he looks into the fire, imagining "the vivid image of Mary's face" (113) and feeling "giddy and hysterical with fear" (114).

Wright clearly establishes the fact that Mary's head, rather than being a naturalistic image merely disclosing Bigger's fear of getting caught, is instead a poetic image arising from the deepest levels of Bigger's moral imagination, telling him that in killing Mary he has in fact killed part of himself. Indeed, Wright has Bigger at one point imagining his own head in the same terms that he had earlier imagined Mary's head. After having been questioned by Britten about what happened the night Mary died and secretly relishing his killing of Mary because it "evened the score" (155) against the white world, Bigger falls asleep and has a dream that runs exactly counter to his coldly amoral thoughts. In this dream he imagines himself carrying a large package in his hands while walking down a dark street. He is alarmed when he hears the "ringing of a distant church bell" (156) and panics when the bell tolls more loudly, seeming to ring "directly above his head" (156). He then runs into an alley, unwraps the package, and discovers in amazement that it contains "his *own* head . . . lying with black face and half-closed eyes" (156). The sounds of the bell get progressively louder, and when Bigger runs away to hide from its noise he finds himself surrounded by white people. The dream concludes with Bigger throwing the severed head into the crowd of whites, cursing them and the bell.

This dream, rendered in a powerful stream of consciousness that exposes Bigger's most private self, establishes that Bigger is no amoral monster who wantonly kills and is incapable of feeling the human implications of his actions. The church bells are clearly a symbol of conscience awakening in Bigger to a pained awareness of the moral consequences of his actions. And he not only feels guilty about having deprived May of life but is also aware, as the discovery of his *own* head in the package suggests, that in killing Mary he has also destroyed part of himself. Bigger's dream, which uses imagery of noise, darkness, and entrapment found in the novel's opening scenes, shows him to be more than a cornered animal because he possesses a moral imagination that is uniquely human.

Bigger's conscience is also powerfully demonstrated with the image of the furnace, an image that also dominates his mind, regardless of how hard he tries to shake it from his awareness. Literally the means by which he disposes of Mary's body, it becomes a symbol of the ethical self that will not let him morally dispose of the consequences of his actions. Although his conscious mind enables him to "blot out" Mary by physically burning her body and then coldly rationalizing his killing of her as an act of rebellion, his subconscious mind impels him to return to the scene of the crime, where he repeatedly examines the furnace, which has become a striking metaphor of his fiery conscience. When Bigger is questioned by reporters and the police, he is acutely aware of the furnace, which "droned and cast huge shadows . . . across the walls" (149). Although his outward behavior is cool and controlled, the self beneath this mask created by Bigger's rational mind is tormented by shadowy feelings of guilt. In a subsequent scene, Bigger is questioned by Jan and Britten and afterward returns to the basement, experiencing "fiery whips of fear and guilt"

(161) as he shakes down the ashes in the furnace. Being interrogated by Britten has touched off Bigger's fears of being caught, but his conversation with Jan has affected Bigger on a deeper level, evoking a sense of remorse that he has difficulty handling. After Bigger drafts an extortion note with Bessie, an action providing him with a conscious satisfaction of gaining control over the Daltons and the white world they represent, he again returns to the basement and sees the furnace as "an enraged beast" throbbing with heat and "suffusing a red glare over everything" (174). Again Wright stresses a powerful duality in Bigger—his conscious self leads him to amorally manipulating others while his subconscious self is driven by a conscience that by now has become an "enraged beast" dominating Bigger by permeating all things with the red glare of his guilt.

The furnace and Mary's head are therefore much more revealing of Bigger's inward life than the white cat that has been so much discussed by the critics. The cat, with its white fur and piercing green eyes, symbolizes the social system that Bigger fears will see his guilt and punish him for his crimes. Sensing himself as a kind of rat, he fears he will be cornered by a natural enemy, the cat, which will then toy with him and destroy him. But the images of the furnace and Mary's head force us to see Bigger as a person, not a rat, because these images go to the core of Bigger's interior life, where we discover that he is indeed human because he is endowed with an active conscience. During the scene in which the furnace erupts with smoke and eventually reveals Bigger as Mary's killer, he actually identifies himself with the furnace: "he himself was a huge furnace now through which no air could go" (205). Choked not only by fear of being caught but also by guilt over what he has done, Bigger will not function well until he has cleared the "smoke" out of his system by coming to human terms with the full implications of his violent actions. In the same way, the image of Mary's bloody head arises from the deepest levels of Bigger's private self and reveals the human impulses that have been stifled by environmental pressures. Ironically, Bigger's head and Mary's head are the same. Bigger's dream vividly reveals that in destroying Mary he has damaged an important part of himself.

Characterization

One of the most extraordinary parts of Wright's depiction of Bigger's character is his drawing of striking human parallels between Bigger and Mary, as victim and attacker become one. Again, Bigger is portrayed as something other than a psychopathic monster; on the contrary, he is revealed as a human being who is driven by an inhuman environment to attack and destroy a woman who in many ways represents important parts of himself.

Throughout books 1 and 2 Bigger and Mary are subtly linked, even though they appear to come from separate universes. Both characters are alienated from their environments and are perceived as aberrant by many of the people who are closest to them. In the novel's opening scene, Bigger's mother becomes so exasperated by his behavior that she calls him "crazy" and warns him about the direction his life is taking: "You'll regret how you living some day. . . . If you don't stop running with that gang of yours and do right you'll end up where you never thought you would" (13). In the same way, Peggy, the Daltons' maid, characterizes Mary as "kind of wild," a well-intentioned but naive girl who worries her folks "to death" by running around with "a wild and crazy bunch of reds" (58). Just as Mrs. Thomas views her son's erratic behavior as a threat to the well-being of their family, Peggy claims that Mary's activities run counter to order and stability in the family: "If it wasn't for Mary and her wild ways, this household would run like a clock" (117). To further reinforce these similarities between the two characters, Mr. Dalton describes Mary as "that crazy daughter of mine" directly after he has characterized Bigger as a sort of "problem boy" (154).

What Wright suggests here by these important parallels is that Bigger and Mary share a common humanity, despite the obvious dissimilarities arising from their radically different social and economic backgrounds. Although this humanity is frustrated in different ways by environment, the same results are produced: alienation and rebellion. Mary's physically comfortable life has given her privileges and opportunities denied to Bigger, but it has also stunted her growth by making her "blind" (102) to reality. Just as Bigger has been walled off from many aspects of life by his stark poverty and his status as a black man in a white world, Mary has been separated from real experience by overly protective parents and her privileged status as a rich white girl. Both respond to their situations in very similar ways—Bigger in forming a gang that engages in acts of rebellion by robbing stores, and Mary by developing friendships with Communists who are committed to overturning society by redistributing wealth. Both characters rebel strongly against the families into which they are born because they sense that these families block their own human development. Because Bigger is "sick of his life at home" (16) he becomes part of a peer group that represents everything of which his mother does not approve. Mary too feels stifled by the limits imposed upon her by her family and deliberately opposes their wishes by running away to New York, taking off with Jan to Florida, and entering his circle of radicals.

Important links are also drawn between Bigger and nearly every other major character in the novel, again stressing that Bigger is a representative man, a "native son" who experiences in extreme form many of the same problems suffered in less apparent ways by people who seem to have nothing in common with him. Like Mr. and Mrs. Dalton, he is portrayed as a "blind" person who is often afraid to face truths about his life for fear that these truths will lead to his undoing. Like Jan and Max, he feels compelled to rebel against an unjust society but is unable to formulate an effective kind of action that will change that society. Like Buckley, Britten, and the social system they represent, he resorts to violence to "blot out" those aspects of reality which he cannot understand and which threaten his sense of well-being.

The connections between Bigger and Bessie are especially strong. Just as his killing of Mary is part of his desire to smother the "soft" side of him that seeks expanded possibilities, because he resents the fact that these possibilities will ultimately be denied to blacks, he kills Bessie because he sees in her another "hard" side of him that is also doomed by environment. For Bigger, Bessie represents that part of him which is trapped by poverty and racial discrimination. He resents Bessie for most of the same reasons he resents other black people, most notably his mother and Reverend Hammond, and he kills Bessie for precisely the same reasons he almost killed Gus in book 1. Although part of Bigger is attracted to Bessie because she offers him relief from the tensions of living in a world dominated by white people like the Daltons, another part of him despises her because he sees in her the same fear, impotence, and despair he also sees inside himself. His desire to "blot out" (119) Bessie is therefore stronger than his impulse to love or even rape her. In the final analysis, he sees Bessie as a mirror into which he can no longer bear to look.

Just as Bigger initially reflected some of Mary's qualities in the scene in Mary's bedroom, he strongly resembles Bessie in the scene in which he murders her. Drinking heavily in the first part of the scene, he becomes strangely lethargic. He complains of feeling "tired and awful sleepy" (212). Although he should be intent on keeping his mind alert and his body ready for escape, he drinks from the whiskey bottle Bessie keeps in her purse. Because "the whiskey lulled him, numbed his senses" (218), it reduces him for the time being to Bessie's level of passivity. The effect is to nullify his impulses to escape: "It seemed that his body had turned into a piece of lead" (212). To underscore further this transformation of Bigger into Bessie, Wright tells us: "Bessie cried again. He caught her face in his hands. He was concerned; he wanted to see this thing through her eyes at that moment" (213). Touching Bessie, Bigger momentarily assumes her perspective, fully assimilating the despair she articulates soon afterward:

> I wish to God I never seen you. I wish one of us had died before we was born. All you ever caused me was trouble, just plain black trouble. . . . I see it now. I ain't drunk now. I see everything you ever did to me. I didn't want to see it before. I was too busy thinking about how good I felt when I was with you. I thought I was happy, but deep down in me I knew I wasn't. But you got me into this murder and I see it all now. I been a fool, just a blind dumb black drunk fool. (215–16).

Bessie, who at this point simply repeats the negative things Bigger's mother has said about him in the novel's opening scene, becomes an externalization not only of Bigger's environment but also of the self-hatred induced by that environment. In this sense, Bigger is driven to kill her and what she represents in an effort "to save himself" (216). Although his conscious mind falsely justifies her murder on the basis that she will physically hinder his escape, his subconscious thinking provides the real motive: Killing her is an attempt to destroy that part of him which is trapped in self-loathing and despair.

Bigger is therefore the novel's "central" character in a very literal way, for nearly all the novel's other characters who surround him reflect various aspects of his personality. The result is Wright's achievement of a complex, multifaceted character who transcends all the simplistic labels that many have applied to him. Wright's hero is indeed "bigger" than the two stereotypes his name immediately calls to mind: the "bad nigger" who defines himself in terms of self-destructive violence and the "Uncle Tom" who suffocates his humanity by acting weakly within the limits of a racist society. Bigger is also more complex than the "boy" Mr. Dalton mistakes him for and the black buck Mary wants him to be. He certainly transcends the categories imposed upon him by Max's ideology, for he is much more than a social "problem" (361); he is a complicated individual with personal drives and needs that political abstractions can never describe or touch. Like Ellison's invisible man, Bigger finally realizes that he is "invisible" to the people around him because they filter their perceptions of him through compulsive feelings that block their vision of him and conveniently reduce him to simpler, more manageable terms. But he is also like Ellison's hero in that he finally overcomes his own "blindness," developing a firm, clear knowledge of his own many-sided identity.

Wright's portrayal of the characters surrounding Bigger, however, tends to be quite different, for these characters are presented in much simpler terms, as "flat," one-dimensional figures rather than fully rounded, three-dimensional persons. Thus Mr. Dalton is a conventional white liberal whose acts of apparent kindness are really rooted in guilt over his exploitative treatment of black people. Buckley and Britten are equally stereotypical white racists who see blacks in brutally inhuman terms because they are blinded by fear and a desire for power. Jan and Max are typical radicals whose responses to life are so much shaped by political ideology that they lack the normal emotions that would enrich their personalities. In the same way, Bigger's brother, Buddy, and his friends, Gus, Jack, and J.H., are seen in very general terms as types but are never probed in detail as individuals.

The women in the novel are especially simplified, and this aspect has resulted in feminist critics recently criticizing Wright for giving a stereotyped account of female experience. Mrs. Thomas is seen as a black matriarch who retreats into conventional religion because she is unable to handle the demands of the real world. Bessie is likewise narcotized by alcohol, swing music, and sex because she is afraid to challenge the white world that dominates her. Mary Dalton, although coming from the opposite end of the social scale and enjoying rights and privileges denied to Bessie and Mrs. Thomas, is also a stereotyped "rich man's daughter" lacking in individualizing traits. Even as she attempts to rebel against her environment, she is victimized by it. Like Bessie, she retreats into alcohol and sex in an attempt to relieve the pressures of an environment she feels stifled by, and like Bessie, she is ultimately destroyed by forces in the environment she does not understand.

What is common to all of the characters who surround Bigger is their lack of a significant inward life that could endow them with the human complexity that makes Bigger such a remarkable character. We see them only from the outside, and their actions seem to imply that they are driven by simple emotions and dominated by external pressures. Each is therefore a passive receptor of environmental stimuli rather than a complex, self-propelling individual.

Wright's purpose in thus simplifying the people around Bigger is to stress the heroic nature of Bigger's achievement of selfhood. In a world that dehumanizes people from all levels of society regardless of economic, social, or educational background, Bigger's journey to self is all the more remarkable. He therefore emerges from the novel as much more than just a "native son," a representative figure symbolizing the plight of modern man. Ultimately, he is a complexly drawn individual, a hero who succeeds where others fail.

8

Point of View

Wright's simplification of the characters surrounding Bigger can also be explained by examining the novel's form, specifically its handling of point of view, the perspective from which the novel is narrated. In 'How Bigger Was Born" Wright emphasizes that in order to provide a more intense and dramatic sense of Bigger's life he decided to tell the story from the perspective of the main character, filtering everything through Bigger's unique angle of vision:

> Wherever possible, I told Bigger's life in close-up, slow motion. I had long had the feeling that this was the best way to "enclose" the reader's mind in a new world, to blot out all reality except that which I was giving him.
>
> Then again, as much as I could, I restricted the novel to what Bigger saw and felt, to the limits of his feeling and thoughts, even when I was conveying *more* than that to the reader. I had the notion that such a manner of rendering made for a sharper effect, a more pointed sense of the character, his peculiar type of being and consciousness. Throughout there is but one point of view: Bigger's. This too, made for a richer illusion of reality.
>
> I kept out of the story as much as possible for I wanted the

reader to feel that there was nothing between him and Bigger; that the story was a *première* given in his own private theatre (xxxii).

Because the novel is thus filtered through the highly pressurized mind of a young person who has been severely conditioned by an environment that limits his awareness of and contacts with people, the people around him are presented to the reader as simplified types rather than fully individualized persons. Bigger's society has put considerable "limits" on his "thoughts and feelings," enclosing him in a rigidly segregated world where he rarely sees white people and when he does so his perception of them is clouded with fear and mistrust. Moreover, this racist society has also divided blacks against one another, weakening the family unit and eroding—with various psychological, economic, and social pressures—a sense of community. Such a doubly divisive society, which walls people off from one another and thus makes them "blind" to one another as human beings, encourages people to regard others as simple stereotypes rather than complex human beings. As we have observed, all the novel's characters, from the highly educated Max to the undereducated Bessie, fall prey to this kind of stereotyping. It would therefore be surprising if Bigger were able to see those around him in richly human terms, as complicated, three-dimensional figures.

Why, then, did Wright choose to filter the novel through the distorting medium of Bigger's mind? Why did he not tell the story through his own omniscient point of view, thereby allowing him to transcend the limits of Bigger's perspective? He also had other options for narration. For example, he might have used a major character at the center of the action to tell the story, an older, more experienced first-person narrator who could present the characters in a more balanced way. Or he could have chosen a first-person outsider narrator like Fitzgerald's Nick Carroway or Conrad's Marlowe, people on the outside of the novel's major events whose finely tuned sensibilities allow them to present a comprehensive and penetrating vision of several characters.

An examination of the form of narration Wright chose for *Native Son*—a point of view technically described as third-person-limited—confirms that Wright knew exactly what he was doing when he worked out the novel's angle of vision. Such a point of view allows the author to use his own voice when telling the story but requires him to limit his vision strictly to the central character's perceptions. As Wright observed in "How Bigger Was Born," such a narrative strategy provides the reader with a sense of realism and immediacy, because we read the story as we live our lives, restricted by the limits of a single point of view. It also promotes an intense bonding between reader and central character, because the reader *assumes* the perspective of the character as he reads the story. These strengths of third-person-limited narration become clearly evident in such scenes as the poolroom fight between Gus and Bigger:

> His face softened a bit and the hard glint in his bloodshot eyes died. But he still knelt with the open knife. Then he stood.
> "Get up!" he said.
> "Please, Bigger!"
> "You want me to slice you?"
> He stooped again and placed the knife at Gus's throat. Gus did not move and his large black eyes looked pleadingly. Bigger was not satisfied; he felt his muscles tightening again. "Get up! I ain't going to ask you no more!"
> Slowly, Gus stood. Bigger held the open blade an inch from Gus's lips.
> "Lick it," Bigger said, body tingling with elation. Gus's eyes filled with tears.
> "Lick it, I said! You think I'm playing?" Gus looked round the room without moving his head, just rolling his eyes in a mute appeal for help. But no one moved. Bigger's left fist was slowly lifting to strike. Gus's lips moved toward the knife; he stuck out his tongue and touched the blade. Gus's lips quivered and tears streamed down his cheeks.
> "Hahahaha!" Doc laughed.
> "Aw leave 'im alone," Jack called.
> Bigger watched Gus with lips twisted in a crooked smile.
> "Say, Bigger ain't you scared 'im enough?" Doc asked.

Bigger did not answer. His eyes gleamed hard again, pregnant
with another idea.

"Put your hands up, way up!" he said

Gus swallowed and stretched his hands high along the wall.

"Leave 'im alone, Bigger," G.H called weakly.

"I'm doing this," Bigger said.

He put the tip of the blade into Gus's shirt and then made an
arc with his arm, as though cutting a circle. (40–41).

Although the scene comes to us through the author's voice, this
voice restricts itself to Bigger's perceptions. We see only what Bigger
sees, we hear only what Bigger hears, and these sensations are presented so that we receive them from Bigger's angle of perception as he
dominates Gus. We do not have the scene as it might be filtered
through Gus's terror or the pool hall owner's anger. But if Bigger
narrated the scene in his *own* voice and thus became a first-person
narrator, either of two things would have happened: (1) If the scene
were described in the present, he would be too agitated to render the
scene in the clear, restrained, and coherent way in which it comes to
us, or (2) if the scene were described in retrospect, it would lack the
dramatic immediacy of a scene unfolding before our eyes in the present
and Bigger might still be unable to grasp its full implications. Like
Dreiser's Carrie Meeber, Fitzgerald's Jay Gatsby, and Conrad's Kurtz,
Bigger lacks the ability to see and understand the full meaning of his
experiences and so his story must be narrated by someone outside
himself. By using third-person narration, Wright can gain some distance from the turbulent world of his central character and use his
own voice to employ language in a very sophisticated way to create a
number of striking effects. These effects would not be achieved if the
central character narrated the scene in his own voice, because he is not
fully aware of the implications of the scene's meaning and also lacks
the language resources to render the scene in a clear and resonant way.
For example, Bigger would not be aware of the connection Wright
makes between him and the rat of the opening scene, but the narrator
makes an important link between Bigger's mode of attack with a sharp
knife and the rat's mode of attack with its equally sharp "fangs" or

"tusks." Bigger would also not be aware of how two other revealing images the narrator weaves into the scene also reverberate throughout the novel, generating meanings that go well beyond the character's understanding. When the reader observes Bigger tormenting Gus by waving a knife in a circular pattern above his chest, he connects the image of the circle with its use in other scenes to suggest that Bigger is trapped in a routine of compulsive activity. Although Bigger believes his violence has freed him of fear and allowed him to gain control over the situation by exercising power over another person, the way in which the scene is rendered suggests that precisely the opposite is the case. Bigger's violence in this scene is part of a pattern of repetition that encircles *him*, making it difficult for him to free himself of environmental conditioning.

The narrator's conscious handling of ocular imagery also suffuses this episode with meanings that Bigger as a first-person narrator would be unlikely to understand. The narrator's emphasis of Bigger's "bloodshot eyes" at the beginning of the scene and his mention of the "hard gleam" in Bigger's eyes at the end of the scene tie in with a pattern of ocular imagery used in other parts of the novel, imagery suggesting that Bigger is not poised in grim determination (as he might think) but, rather is blinded by self-destructive emotions.

Third-person-limited narration, as Wright pointed out in "How Bigger Was Born," can therefore dramatize the unique perspective of a central character while "conveying *more* than that to a reader" (xxxxii). By using the author's sophisticated literary voice, it can create subtle effects that transcend the limited awareness of the central character. Such a point of view has some of the clarity of omniscient narration without distancing the reader excessively and sacrificing immediacy. It also has some of the intensity and directness of first-person narration without becoming overly subjective and sacrificing clarity. This narrative perspective was ideally suited for Wright's purposes in *Native Son* because he wanted (1) to center his story on a character who was too inarticulate and submerged in turbulent experiences to tell his own story effectively but also (2) to tell that story in a powerfully immediate way so that the reader would be "enclosed" in a "new world." the world of the ghetto as perceived firsthand by one of its victims.

It would have been far easier for Wright to have told Bigger's story using the omniscient narration of previous black novels like Dunbar's *The Sport of the Gods* and McKay's *Home to Harlem,* because this kind of strategy would have allowed him to view Bigger's explosive world from the safe remove of a godlike author. Or he could have narrated the novel in an excessively personal way using the confessional first-person point of view found in Johnson's *The Autobiography of an Ex-Colored Man.* Because Wright rejected these conventional options in favor of an aesthetically demanding but deeply expressive third-person point of view, he was able to make *Native Son* a revolutionary novel, a landmark in American fiction. *Native Son* is the first novel to focus sharply on the experiences of an undereducated, embittered black man growing up in a smoldering ghetto and to relate his experiences *from his unique perspective,* all the white suggesting rich meanings that go well beyond that character's field of vision. Like Twain's *Adventures of Huckleberry Finn, Native Son* uses point of view masterfully to open up a new way of looking at important aspects of American experience.

An essential part of Bigger's perspective is his unique manner of picturing the white world. Never before had an American novel portrayed in such a bold, uncompromisingly honest way the deep sense of exclusion blacks felt from mainstream America and their sense of the white world as a strange and hostile environment. To make us experience Bigger's point of view toward whites, Wright develops striking patterns of imagery suggesting that, for one in Bigger's position, it is almost impossible to perceive whites as human beings. Bigger often sees whites in grotesquely stylized terms, for example, perceiving Mrs. Dalton as a "ghost" (48) and Mary as "a doll in a show window" (63). Driving in the car with Jan and Mary, he feels as if "he was sitting between two vast white looming walls" (68). Late in the novel he envisions Buckley as a "white mountain looming" (276) over him. Bigger regularly sees whites in such terms, as vast, impersonal forces that "loom over" him, diminishing him, threatening his life:

To Bigger and his kind white people were not really people; they were a sort of great natural force, like a stormy sky looming overhead, or like a deep swirling river stretching suddenly at one's feet in the dark. As long as he and his black folks did not go beyond certain limits, there was no need to fear that white force. But whether they feared it or not, each and every day of their lives they lived with it; even when words did not sound its name, they acknowledged its reality. As long as they lived here in this prescribed corner of the city, they paid mute tribute to it. (109)

Wright also uses ocular imagery in a special way to intensify our feeling for Bigger's alienated perspective. Realizing that there are "certain limits" black people must not go beyond, Bigger is hesitant to establish eye contact with whites, for fear of contacting them on a personal level that they might resent. In his first meeting with Mr. and Mrs. Dalton he is careful not to look directly at them and instead "glare[s] at the floor" (53) during their conversation. He also feels a vague sense of guilt when he looks at Mary during their first meeting and hopes her father has not detected his glimpse of her. When in the car with Mary later that night, Bigger looks at her only through the rearview mirror. When he is forced by Jan's insistence to shake hands, he does so while cocking his head at "an oblique angle" (67) so that he can see him but then shift his vision "out into the street whenever he did not wish to meet Jan's gaze" (67). Indeed, there are only two times in book 1 when Bigger deliberately looks directly into the face of a white person: when he gets angry at Mary as she insists that he enter Ernie's Chicken Shack with her and later when he stares into her face after she has died. Bigger will therefore establish eye contact with whites only after anger has overcome the fear that inhibits him or when he is certain that Mary's eyes, which "bulged glassily" (86), will not return his gaze.

The implications behind this pattern of ocular imagery are quite clear. Bigger feels alienated from a social environment that will punish him both for looking at things in a clear, direct way and for initiating human contact with whites. He is therefore forced to develop the perverse habit of looking at people from a very limited perspective, offering him an extremely distorted vision of the people around him. So deeply engrained is his habit of turning his eyes away from whites that he also extends this habit to his viewing of black people. In the novel's opening scene he averts his eyes from various members of his family and at the end of the scene regards them from behind the "curtain" (14) he has constructed in his mind to snatch glances at people while remaining invisible to them. After he and Bessie make love, Bigger is described as "gazing with vacant eyes at the shadowy ceiling" (129) while she tries to talk to him. When Reverend Hammond talks to Bigger late in the novel, Bigger "stare[s] unblinkingly at the white wall" (263).

Another pattern of imagery that allows us to experience Bigger's point of view as an outsider is the tactile imagery that dramatizes Bigger's unusual fear of touching or being touched by other people. Just as he is hesitant to extablish eye contact with Jan, he is also reluctant to shake hands with him and does so only when Jan insists. He later remembers touching Jan as "that awful moment of hate and shame" (94). While in Mary's bedroom Bigger's frenzy is induced when he thinks that Mrs. Dalton will not only "discover" but "touch" (84) him. When Bessie asks him why he was so frightened of a frail, blind person like Mrs. Dalton, he tells her that "I was scared she was going to touch me" (213). Shortly after discovering that Mary is dead, he has trouble disposing of her body because "he did not want to touch her" (88). When Bessie in a later scene tries to reassure Bigger of her feelings toward him, she "grab[s] his hand and squeeze[s] it" but Bigger [draws] his hand away" (139) because he is uncomfortable with the human contact she initiates. And Bigger's hopeless position at the end of book 2 is depicted by the fact that his hands are literally frozen by the jets of water the police use to immobilize him.

The only times in the first two books when Bigger is able to touch people are in acts of violence. He terrifies Gus in the poolroom by forcing Gus to lick the sharp point of his knife; he suffocates Mary by pressing a pillow to her face; and he crushes Bessie's skull with a brick. Because of his deeply alienated perspective, Bigger shrinks from people and feels a need to "blot out" those around him rather than "see" or "touch" them. In his first meeting with Mr. Dalton his anxieties build to a point where his "impulses were deadlocked" (49) and he "wanted to wave his hand and blot out the white man who was making him feel this way" (50). Riding with Jan and Mary, he instinctively recoils from their physical proximity to him in such an enclosed space, and this feeling of revulsion leads to a desire to annihilate everything around him: "Suddenly he wanted to seize some heavy object in his hand and grip it with all the strength of his body and in some strange way rise up in naked space above the speeding car and with one final blow blot it out—with himself and them in it" (70).

Bigger's urge to destroy extends not only to white people but to himself and other black people. When he wakes up the morning after Mary's death, he looks at his family sleeping in the room with him and wishes "to wave his hand and blot them out" because "they were always too close to him" (95). Shortly thereafter he wants to "blot out" (106) his brother when Buddy offers to help him. Later when he feels a desire for solidarity with black people but considers the difficulties in bringing this about, his impulse to unite with his people sours; he "wanted to wave his hand and blot them out" (109). Although he visits Bessie to establish human contact after his dealings with whites have induced in him a considerable amount of fear and alienation, his moments of intimacy with her nearly always result in Bigger's wanting to destroy her. After being questioned by Mrs. Dalton concerning Mary's whereabouts, Bigger visits Bessie and while walking with her "yearned suddenly to be back in bed with her, feeling her warm and pliant body next to his" (133). But in the very next moment he is overcome by a strong urge to "clench his fist" and "blot out" (133) Bessie. He does exactly this in book 3, after having sex with her. Again, Bigger's alienated state of consciousness explodes in violence when he is emotionally threatened by human contact.

Another powerful way in which Wright gets the reader to experience Bigger's alienated point of view directly is by using images of coldness to suggest how Bigger senses the white world as both separate from and hostile to him. Bigger first perceives the Dalton's neighborhood as "a cold and distant world" (45), and as his conflicts with white people deepen, the weather gets progressively colder. Whereas Gus and Bigger enjoy the uncharacteristic warmth of a bright winter afternoon early in the novel as they hang around the city streets, Bigger notices on the evening before he reports to work at the Daltons that the weather has become ominously colder: "Outside his window he saw the sun dying over the rooftops in the western sky and watched the first shade of dusk fall. . . . All day long it had been springlike; but now the dark clouds were slowly swallowing the sun" (44). Working for the Daltons will not be a rebirth for Bigger, as the earlier "springlike" weather might have suggested. Rather, it will bring on death, as the dark, cold weather emphasizes. From this point on, the "sun" that might have nourished Bigger has died and he is forced to confront a hostile environment that threatens his life. Nearly all the major scenes that take place in the remainder of the novel occur at night while it is snowing. As this snow builds up, Bigger's alienation gradually deepens because he feels surrounded by a world that literally blurs his vision and threatens him with death. Riding at night with Jan and Mary, Bigger looks out the car window and notices snow clouds developing. At the end of book 1 when Bigger is "chilled" by the "cold facts" (88) of his situation, he notices that the weather has grown "colder" and a "few fine flakes of snow" (92) are falling. When he wakes up the next morning and looks out his window, he observes that "snow was falling and an icy wind blew" (95). Bigger later reports to work at the Dalton's house, and, as he drives to the Loop to pick up Mary's trunk, the snow is falling so heavily that he "could not see ten feet in front of him" (145).

This pattern of imagery culminates in two crucial scenes in which Bigger's vision of the white world is dramatized with snow imagery; when he almost kills Jan and when he escapes from the Dalton house. Again Wright's use of the third-person-point of view forces us to assume Bigger's perspective in a dramatic way, seeing as he sees, feeling as he feels, and thinking as he thinks. In "How Bigger Was Born" Wright stressed, "If a thing was cold, I tried to make the reader *feel* cold and not just tell about it" (xxxi). His use of point of view in these two scenes accomplished this task brilliantly.

When Bigger is confronted by Jan outside the Dalton home shortly after he has tried to create suspicion about Jan, we see the episode through Bigger's fiercely alienated mind, not through Jan's puzzled awareness. As the two talk, "huge wet flakes of snow" fall, forming "a delicate screen" (162) between them. This cold physical barrier not only suggests that the two come from separate social universes but also reveals the "curtain" of fear inside Bigger's segregated mind. Such fear blinds him to Jan as a human being but also protects him from any demands Jan might make on him. As Jan inadvertently intensifies Bigger's fear and guilt by insisting they have a cup of coffee and talk about the events of the previous evening, Bigger suddenly erupts, threatening Jan with his gun. The scene ends with Bigger lost in a "strange spell" (162) similar to the one he experienced in Mary's bedroom. Because this scene is narrated through a third-person point of view that makes us assume Bigger's perspective, we understand what kind of "spell" Bigger is under and experience it with him. Had Wright chosen to narrate the scene omnisciently we would have got a more detailed and objective view of things but been at too great a distance from Bigger to feel his plight. As written, the scene powerfully re-creates Bigger's consciousness with a few well-chosen images of snow and darkness.

Bigger's perception of whites as "snow" that blurs his vision and limits his actions is most vividly dramatized when he escapes from the Dalton house after the police and reporters have discovered Mary's bones in the furnace. Seeking to remove himself from a hot, smoky environment that has now become a trap, he jumps into an equally confining environment of coldness:

> He turned to the window and put his hand under the upper ledge and lifted; he felt a cold rush of air laden with snow. . . . Then he leaped headlong, sensing his body twisting in the city air as he hurtled. His eyes were shut and his hands were clenched as his body turned, sailing through the snow. He was in the air a moment; then he hit. It seemed at first that he hit softly, but the shock of it went through him, up his back to his head, and he lay buried in a cold pile of snow, dazed. Snow was in his mouth, eyes, ears; snow was seep-

ing down his back. His hands were wet and cold. Then he felt all of
the muscles of his body contract violently, caught in one spasm of
reflex action, and at the same time he felt his groin laved with warm
water. It was his urine. (207)

Most of the images Wright has used to make us experience Bigger's
alienated point of view appear in this very rich moment. Hurtling
through the air, Bigger shuts his eyes in fear and clenches his fists in
anger. Because he is suspended in the icy air, he has no control over the
natural forces that condition him. Blinded and unable to grasp anything either to direct his movements or to cushion his fall, he once
again enters a strange no-man's land that threatens to blot him out. As
he hits the ground, the physical sensations he experiences become an
epiphany of how he has always experienced the white world. Bigger is
"shocked" and "dazed" by the coldness of the snow just as he has
been numbed by the emotional coldness of people like Mrs. Dalton
and Britten. Furthermore, snow saturates him, literally filling his
mouth, ears, and eyes to suggest the way in which whites like Mary
and Jan have invaded parts of himself that he wants to keep separate
from them.

The effect of all this is for Bigger to erupt in "a spasm of reflex
action" when he hits the ground and urinates on himself. This occur-
rence is quite similar to the kind of self-destructive reflex action that
overcame Bigger in Mary's bedroom and also resulted in his nearly
killing Jan. Bigger at this point is once again confronted with the two
options he has faced in many key parts of the novel: (1) He can
succumb to a hostile environment and be first "soiled" and then "frozen" by it or (2) he can set himself in opposition to this environment
and protect his life. He chooses the latter option when he becomes
aware of what the snow has done to him and then struggles to gain
conscious control over it: "He had not been able to control the muscles of his hot body against the chilled assault of the wet snow over all
his skin. He lifted his head, blinking his eyes, and looked above him.
He sneezed. He was himself now; he struggled against the snow, pushing it away from him. He got to his feet, one at a time, and pulled

himself out. He walked, then tried to run" (207). By "blinking his eyes" he can overcome his dazed condition and then search for a way out of his trap. Because he consciously "struggle[s] against the snow," he becomes something other than what this freezing environment wants him to be, a soiled, immobilized mass of flesh capable only of reflex actions. Opening his eyes, directing his previously stunned body, and consciously pushing the snow away from him, he can begin to function like a person: "He was himself now."

Ironically, one of the few ways in which the Bigger Thomas of books 1 and 2 can get a sense of "himself" is through acts of violence. Although readers have often critized Wright's depiction of Bigger's violence, claiming that it reduces the character to a stereotyped beast, *from Bigger's point of view,* violence is sometimes a way of avoiding being "frozen" by the white world. Violence seems to give him two important human capabilities denied to him by a cold, dark environment—action and awareness. It is in this sense that Bigger feels his killing of Mary has produced a new stage in his life, wherein "the ice was broken" and he can now "do other things" (101). As he mulls over his killing of Mary the next day, he therefore feels that violence has revealed "the hidden meaning of his life" (101), for it has enabled him to strike out against "a world he feared" (101) and such action has freed him to envision himself and his world in a new way. Indeed, he sees his act of violence as equivalent to a religious conversion:

> He had murdered and created a new life for himself. It was something that others could not take from him. Yes; he could sit here calmly and eat and not be concerned about what his family thought or did. He had a natural wall from behind which he could look at them. His crime was an anchor weighing him safely in time; it added to him a certain confidence which his gun and knife did not. He was outside of his family now, over and beyond them; they were incapable of even thinking that he had done such a deed. And he had done something which even they had not thought possible. (101)

Many critics wrongly interpret this passage and others like it as Wright's glorification of violence, not realizing that the scene is narrated through a third-person-limited, not an omniscient, point of view. Although the voice narrating the scene is the author's, the consciousness through which the scene is filtered is Bigger's. It is important to realize, then, that the thoughts Bigger contemplates are his, not Wright's. As is the case in many of the novel's key scenes, Wright's implied attitudes are quite different from his character's explicit attitudes because they come from an outlook that is broader than the character's outlook at this point in his life. Although Wright uses this scene to reinforce once again his criticism of a pathological society that pushes a person to violence as an alternative to paralysis, he does not endorse violence itself. Given the context of the whole novel, Bigger's killing of Mary has not provided him with a new life at all but will in fact seal his doom. Wright also makes it clear that Bigger's violence has not led him to anything really new, because his old life has been filled with similar, though less extreme, acts of violence. His killing of Mary, then, does not represent a dramatic break from an "old" life; rather, it flows naturally from prior events, such as his near killing of Gus.

Although Wright as author does not fully endorse Bigger's perspective on violence at this point in the novel, he does understand the logic behind such a perspective and sees some truth in it, although not the kind of truth Bigger arrives at. Even if Wright rejects the idea that Bigger's killing of Mary has not provided Bigger with a "new life," he does believe that such a violent act exposes the "hidden meaning" (101) of Bigger's old life. Bigger's terrible act reveals that he has always lived in a culture of physical, economic, and moral violence, a culture that has deprived him of a father and also twisted his inward feelings to such an extent that he has enormous difficulty touching people in love but gains deep satisfaction from touching them in hatred. Such a culture, which makes it nearly impossible for Bigger at this point in his life to see himself and others in human terms, imposes two impoverishing "rhythms" on his life, "indifference and violence" (31).

Wright also sees another partial truth in Bigger's claim that violence has given him a new kind of power: "The whole thing came to him in the form of a powerful and simple feeling; there was in everyone a great hunger to believe that made him blind, and if he could see while others were blind, then he could get what he wanted and never be caught at it. Now, who would ever think that he, a black timid Negro boy, would murder and burn a rich white girl and would sit and wait for breakfast like this? Elation filled him" (102). As Wright will emphatically point out before we get far into book 2, Bigger's "elation" is short-lived because his intense feelings of guilt at having destroyed another human being will quickly dissolve such feelings of well-being. Then too, Bigger's mask of a "black timid Negro boy" will collapse when Mary's bones are discovered and another mask will be imposed upon him by white society—the mask of the black beast who must be killed to protect civilization. Violence is again seen by Wright as producing intense emotional satisfaction in the short run but human tragedy in the long run. But Bigger's point of view here, however wrong in the literal sense, nevertheless contains an important truth for Wright, that *genuine* human vision can be a source of power leading to identity. If Bigger can *really* "see" while others are "blind," then he can indeed "get what he wanted." First, though, he has to transform his desires so that what he wants is not the murder of others but a truly humane identity for himself.

In book 3 this change occurs. It is here that Bigger stops gloating over killing Bessie and Mary and comes to terms with the guilt that has been bubbling up from his subconscious mind. As a result, his point of view changes drastically, lessening the distance between his way of seeing things and the author's implied perspective. Bigger finally does achieve a "new life" that Wright endorses, but it is quite different from the conversion he thinks he has undergone as a result of killing Mary and Bessie. A revealing key to this development is his desire and ability to touch others. Although book 2 ends with his hand metaphorically and literally frozen, the final book contains several important scenes in which Bigger makes meaningful contact with himself and others. Encouraged by Jan and Max "to believe in himself," he begins "holding his life in his hands" (288). Observing a fellow black prisoner being manhandled by guards, he feels genuine "sympathy" (318) and a desire to reach out to another human being: "For the first time since his capture, Bigger felt that he wanted someone near him, something physical to cling to" (319). On a broader level, Bigger is able to experience a vision of human solidarity in which all people "touch" one another:

> Slowly he lifted his hands in darkness and held them in mid-air, the fingers spread weakly open. If he reached out with his hands, and if his hands were electric wires, and if his heart were a battery giving life and fire to those hands, and if he reached out with his hands and touched other people, reached out through these stone walls and felt other hands connected with other hearts—if he did that, would there be a reply, a shock? . . . And in that touch, response of recognition, there would be union, identity; there would be a supporting oneness, a wholeness which had been denied him all his life (335).

Here Bigger is no longer divided into two mutually exclusive selves. As a result of this momentary wholeness, he can tentatively reach out to the world in love rather than violence. Although Bigger's efforts to touch people will finally be canceled out by the "shock" of his being executed in the electric chair, Wright nevertheless stresses that Bigger in book 3 achieves a range of human responses not possible for him previously.

Clear evidence of this development is Bigger's changed view of most of the people he had earlier wanted to "blot out." He finally overcomes the feelings of shame and resentment he had previously felt toward his mother and at the end of the novel asks Max to tell her "not to worry none" because he is "all right" (392). Listening to Jan reveal his deepest feelings about Mary, he grasps Jan's humanity and feels genuine remorse for hurting him: "For the first time in his life a white man became a human being to him; and the reality of Jan's humanity came [to him] in a stab of remorse" (268). He likewise identifies with Jan as he is baited on the witness stand by Buckley, sensing a basic kinship with Jan as an outsider to American society. And part of him comes to realize that his killing of Bessie and Mary is no cause for pride. Rather, he begins to understand that his acts stemmed from his own "blindness," which resulted in his harming other people and himself:

Another impulse rose in him, born of desperate need, and his mind clothed it in an image of a strong blinding sun sending hot rays down and he was standing in the midst of a vast crowd of men, white men and black men and all men, and the sun's rays melted away the differences, the colors, the clothes, and drew what was common and good toward the sun. . . .

Had he killed Mary and Bessie and brought sorrow to his mother and sister and put himself in the shadow of the electric chair only to find out this? Had he been blind all along? (335)

Bigger's human awareness is never adequate fully to resolve all his problems, because he is never given sufficient time to sustain and develop such an awareness. But Wright does portray him as moving away from the dehumanized violence and impoverished consciousness that characterized his point of view in books 1 and 2. Through the depth of his own suffering and genuine contact with other people, Bigger is able to 'see" much of what he was earlier blind to. He comes to understand that his mother, Jan, Bessie, and Mary are victims of the same society that has brutalized him, and he responds to them with compassion rather than defensive hatred. He also realizes that he killed two people not out of any heroic motives but simply because he was "scared and mad" (328). Moreover, he consciously tries to reconcile his blind feelings with an existential consciousness that can assimilate, transform, and direct those feelings: "He felt he could not move again unless he swung out from the base of his own feelings; he felt he would have to have light in order to act now" (289). Because he makes such a conscious attempt to move from "blind impulses" to "understanding" (334), he begins to live in "a thin, hard core of consciousness" (333).

Although Bigger's newly developed consciousness never quite becomes the same as Wright's implied consciousness as third-person narrator, the distance between the two diminishes considerably by the end of the novel. As this diminishing happens, the authorial voice and the central character's perspective collaborate to produce a vision of life that can be described as both affirmative and ironic. Bigger's final conversations with Max, Jan, and his mother clearly establish that he has developed a balanced, humane point of view. But his "faint wry bitter smile" described in the novel's final paragraph also reveals that he is fully aware of the ironic gap between his own humane vision and the way society continues to operate, for he knows society will execute him precisely at that point in his life where he has achieved human selfhood.

9

Tone

The novel's unique point of view helps create a tone that is consistently ironic. As we have seen, sharp ironies are often produced by the discrepancy between Bigger's explicit views and the author's implied attitudes. After Bigger has seen a film about upper-class whites, he thinks the film has given him new insights about white people that will lead to "something big" (36) because he can now discover how they make money and dominate society. But Wright's implied attitudes make it ironically clear to the reader that the film has given Bigger a number of misleading stereotypes that will blind him to the true nature of whites and cause him real trouble later on. Likewise, Bigger thinks his extortion plot will give him money and power, but Wright's narrative voice undercuts his views with blatant ironies because Bigger's plan is so crudely envisioned and executed that it is bound to blow up in his face. In the same way, when Bigger is tricked by Buckley into signing his confession he thinks such an act will make him feel better, but Wright presents the scene as a cheap betrayal of Bigger that results in his feeling even worse about himself, for after he has signed the confession and realized how he has been manipulated by Buckley, he feels "empty and beaten" (288).

Irony is also produced from Bigger's own perspective as he continually observes a wide gap between the democratic promises of American life and the harsh realities around him. This kind of irony is particularly evident in an early scene in which Bigger and Gus hang around the streets and consider their opportunities as black people in a white-dominated society. Bigger is fascinated with the movement he detects in the world around him because he instinctively associates this movement with expanded possibilities leading to human growth. As he watches the clouds drift by, the cars whirring through the streets, and people walking about, the narrator tells us, "Every movement in the street evoked a casual curiosity in him" (19). Bigger's deepest yearnings are evoked when he spots a plane overhead skywriting the word "USE." Although he would like to "use" his life productively by becoming a pilot, he knows Gus is right when he reminds Bigger that such "flying" is reserved for whites. Bigger realizes he will never get a chance to use his talents, and so he cultivates an essentially ironic view of American life.

This ironic view is dramatized powerfully when he and Gus "play white" (21) shortly after they have discussed the plane flying overhead. Parodying the roles of generals directing armies, J. P. Morgan dominating the business world, and the president of the United States organizing a cabinet meeting, they "leaned against the wall and laughed" (22). Although this game makes them fully aware of their impotence in a white-dominated society, the rich ironies they enjoy as they enact the roles of whites gives them a way of psychologically coping with their situation, for such irony not only results in laughter-producing awareness but also enables them to translate their anger into a kind of social protest. As Bigger enacts the role of president, he indirectly articulates his anger about being black in a white-dominated society:

> "Well, you see, the niggers is raising sand all over the country," Bigger said, struggling to keep back his laughter. "We've got to do something with these black folks."
>
> "Oh if it's about the niggers, I'll be right there, Mr. President," Gus said. (22)

The ironies of this scene closely resemble those found in the blues, a form of black folk art Wright admired for its "paradoxical" ability to make "an almost exultant affirmation of life" even while carrying a "burden of woe and melancholy."[26] Like the blues singer, Bigger is able to look at the painful facts of his situation as a black person victimized by a racist society, frankly observing, "We black and they white" (23), and "They don't let us do *nothing*" (22). But like the blues musician, he can also cope with his situation and to some extent psychologically master it through an act of ironic awareness, for blues irony produces both laughter, which transforms pain into pleasure, and awareness, which gives the underdog a psychological weapon to use against his oppressors. As Ralph Ellison observed, the blues have a "sheer toughness of spirit"[27] that enables blacks not only to survive American racism but to overcome some of its psychological burdens. When Gus and Bigger "play white," they clearly exhibit this toughness of spirit, turning a condition of physical oppression into a state of ironic awareness.

Blues ironies resonate throughout *Native Son,* from its very first words to its final image. The novel's title establishes the central character as a representative American figure who desires to achieve the American dream but who has to live an American nightmare because history has excluded him from the mainstream of American life. And the novel's final sentence describes Bigger's "faint, wry, bitter, smile" (392) as he considers the ironic fact that Max, whose political convictions commit him to a belief in universal brotherhood, cannot translate such ideas into action in the real world by simply turning around and confronting Bigger face to face as a human being. Similarly, most of the novel's major characters are named in a way that reinforces the novel's ironic tone. As we have seen, Bigger's first and last names call to mind the stereotypes of "Uncle Tom" and "nigger," but his portrayal in the novel ironically establishes him as a human being who transcends these stereotypes, even though almost none of the people around him are aware of this transcendence. The Daltons are ironically named after a form of color blindness called Daltonism. Although they see themselves as good liberal people who are "color-blind" in the positive sense of being without racial prejudice, the novel establishes them as "color-blind" in the negative sense, for it reveals that they are tragically blind to the way a white system oppresses blacks and how they as slumlords are part of the problem. Bigger's brother is named Buddy to suggest a close personal relationship, but in fact the two are strangers to each other because ghetto life has divided members of the black family against one another, separating them with "walls" of fear and mistrust. Mary Dalton's first name might initially suggest a parallel with the mother of Christ, but the allusion is bitterly ironic because she is neither a virgin nor a person who can offer Bigger redemptive love; on the contrary, the "love" she offers Bigger leads him to his doom. Jan Erlone's name is also heavily ironic. Although he sees himself as a sort of Janus figure who will lead people to a new world of brotherhood, he is unable even to overcome his own condition—suggested by his last name—of being alone. The ideology that has promised to give him a sense of solidarity with the masses has ironically set him apart from others, making him a sort of pariah.

Given the novel's overall tone of irony, it is not surprising that many of its central scenes are powerfully ironic inversions of conventional scenes from traditional literature; that is, they use motifs from these scenes but turn their meanings inside out, producing effects exactly the opposite of those contained in the original scenes. Bigger's killing of Mary Dalton, for example, is a remarkable inversion of a love scene from a romantic novel. This scene—perhaps the most revealing one Wright ever wrote—ironically describes violence in terms of romantic lovemaking to suggest that Bigger's creative and destructive drives have been snarled, locking him in a psychological trap that suffocates his deepest human impulses. The episode begins in a simple, erotic way, with Mary attempting to arouse Bigger sexually. In the car she tells him he is "very nice," deliberately sprawls her legs "wide apart" (80), and leans her head on his shoulder. When she catches him looking at her exposed legs, she laughs and asks him to carry her out of the car, while her "dark eyes looked feverishly at him" (81). Although she is somewhat intoxicated, she is much more in control of herself than she allows Bigger to realize. Swaying against him, she asks him to take her up the "back way" (82) to her room. Although she is surely conscious enough to give him directions and reject his advances if she wishes, she does not resist "the tips of his fingers feeling the soft swell of her breasts" (82). Indeed, she clearly desires to make love to him, her world's forbidden fruit. As he carries her up the stairs, "she pulled heavily on him, her arm around his neck" (82) and her hair brushing his lips. Fully aroused now, Bigger feels "possessed" (83) by her, *his* world's forbidden fruit.

Several erotic images are then used to describe the two entering Mary's room. As his fingers spread over Mary's back "her face came toward him and her lips touched his" (84). Although he wants to leave after he has "laid" (84) her on the bed, he is overtaken by sexual desires. When he tightens his fingers on her breasts and kisses her twice, she moves toward him, clearly encouraging his actions.

Mrs. Dalton's entry into the room abruptly turns their love-making into death-making. But Wright artfully persists in using erotic images to describe the scene, turning them inside out for shockingly ironic effect. As Mrs. Dalton approaches them, all of Bigger's violent tendencies become "erected": "he grew tight and full, as though about to explode" (84). When Mary's fingernails tear at him, he covers her entire face with a pillow, and her suffocation is described in terms of copulation: "Mary's body surged upward and he pushed downward upon the pillow with all of his weight, determined that she must not move or make any sound that would betray him. . . . Again Mary's body heaved and he held the pillow in a grip that took all of his strength. For a long time he felt the sharp pain of her fingernails biting into his wrists" (84–85). After her "surging and heaving" (85) body finally relaxes and Mrs. Dalton leaves the room, Bigger orgasmically utters "a long gasp" (85). In the afterglow of this strange experience, he is depicted as "weak and wet with sweat" (85), listening for some time to his heavy breathing filling the darkness.

Bigger's reaction to his killing Mary can likewise be seen as an ironic reversal of the sort of "conversion" experience depicted in Christian tradition dating back to St. Augustine's *Confessions*. Although such religious conversions depict a dramatic moment of awakening in which a person turns from an "old" life that has trapped him in sin to a "new" life that cleanses him of sin and points the way to redemption, Bigger's killing of Mary is not a dramatic change in his character but instead, the culmination of violent tendencies that have been boiling in him for a long time. When Bigger thinks "he had murdered and created a new life for himself" (101), his thought is ironically undercut by the fact that such a "murder" will lead directly to his death in the electric chair rather than to a new life. Likewise, Bigger is wrong when he sees himself as undergoing a baptism through his killing of Mary. Such violence does not make him "like a man reborn" and it does not make him "like a man risen up from a long illness" (106); instead, his acts of violence come from the "old" Bigger, a person made sick by a pathological society intent on destroying him.

The novel's final scene is also a revealing inversion of the endings of conventional gangster movies and crime stories appearing in popular magazines. As Ross Pudaloff and others have pointed out, Wright was fascinated by popular films and was also an avid reader of such magazines as *Argosy All-Story Magazine* and *Flynn's Detective Weekly,* which featured sensationalistic stories about hideous crimes being solved and criminals being justly punished for such crimes.[28] In writing the ending of *Native Son,* Wright consciously used many of the conventions of popular films and stories about crime but inverted them for subtly ironic effect. He rejects altogether the simple moralistic allegory that prevails in popular films and detective fiction in favor of a much more complex and ironic vision. The popular crime literature of Wright's day always presents execution as an appropriate punishment for "murderers" and suggests that society is cleansed when it destroys such people, who are a threat to the social order. But as Wright presents the ending of *Native Son,* society has wrongly condemned a man to death for two reasons: (1) Legally, it has convicted him of crimes he did not commit, since Bigger did not rape Mary and his killing of her was accidental, and (2) morally, such a punishment is not justified, because Bigger is not a pathological monster who is a threat to the social order but a person who has undergone a profound psychological change that has cleansed him of his compulsion for violence. Because society's killing of Bigger cannot be justified on either legal or moral grounds, Wright ironically links society's actions with Bigger's earlier killings of Mary and Bessie. All three deaths take place when intimate human activity is initiated but is then aborted by environmentally induced fear and hatred. Just as Bigger's and Mary's lovemaking is inverted into killing when Mrs. Dalton strikes terror into Bigger's heart, Bessie is murdered when Bigger's attempts to "love" her are overcome by his fear that she will somehow reveal his whereabouts to the police. In a comparable way, the serious conversation begun by Bigger and Max at the end of the novel is cut off by Max's terror, Bigger's incomplete understanding, and society's fear that real human bonds might eventually develop between two such hated people. *Native Son* therefore concludes with the same brutal irony that has vibrated throughout the novel: Death comes precisely at the threshold of our most deeply human experiences. This finally becomes Wright's most terrible revelation of a social world that encourages and even necessitates fear and hatred but violently blocks love and understanding wherever it emerges. Drawing upon popular films and stories that formulaically conclude with reassuring allegorical scenes equating criminals with evil and society with goodness, Wright transforms these materials, ending his novel with provocative ironies that force us to think well beyond the clichés of popular art.

Wright not only used such ironic inversions in key scenes but also employed broader patterns of irony throughout the novel. His handling of Christian imagery and symbolism is a particularly good example. Wright, who was brought up in part by a grandmother who was deeply committed to fundmentalist religion, rebelled strongly against conventional Christianity at a very early age, but he consciously used Christian motifs, usually for ironic purposes, in all his major fiction. This is particularly true of *Native Son*. From the very beginning of the novel the conventional religion practiced by Bigger's mother is ironically juxtaposed against the harsh realities the Thomas family has to face. Rather than helping her cope with these harsh realities, the religion practiced by Mrs. Thomas encourages her to escape to a world of illusion that temporarily enables her to feel better but in the long run makes her problems worse. At the end of the novel's first scene, which portrays the Thomas family trapped by a racist environment, Mrs. Thomas sings a spiritual that envisions life as a liberating journey directed by a powerful and benevolent God. But while the song imagines human life as a "mountain railroad" controlled by an "engineer" who helps people make "the run successful from cradle to grave" (14), the actual circumstances of the Thomas family ironically contradict this uplifting view, for since the death of Bigger's father in a southern race riot, nobody has been able to direct the family in any effective way. As a result, their life has been anything but a smoothly run journey and they have alternated between utter paralysis and purposeless drifting. The song "irked" (14) Bigger because he sees its affirmative imagery as a bleak contrast to his family's actual situation. He also is annoyed a few minutes later when his mother says grace at breakfast, thanking the Lord for "the food you done placed before us for the nourishment of our bodies" (14). Ironically, the only food they can afford to eat will give them little nourishment, consisting as it does of small amounts of coffee, bacon, and bread. Bigger therefore sees his mother's otherworldly religion as a cruel joke and often identifies such religion with the whiskey Bessie consumes, because both are palliatives that allow people to withdraw from reality, all the while eroding their will to change reality.

Whenever Bigger confronts the sort of religion his mother practices he responds to it in a bitterly ironic way. After he hears his mother saying during her evening prayers, "Lord, I want to be a Christian in my heart" (37), he immediately goes to his room, takes his gun from under his mattress, and puts it inside his shirt. While conventional Christianity reminds Bigger of his family's impotence and resignation, his gun provides him with a sense of power. In book 2 he likewise rejects the otherworldly religion he observes black people practicing during a church service. As he listens to them singing "Stealaway to Jesus" (237–38) he consciously rejects such passivity and "surrender" (237). He instead defines himself in terms of violent rebellion, refusing to surrender to the police and resolving to use his gun rather than prayer as a means of coping with his difficulties. He rejects Reverend Hammond's Christianity in book 3 for the same reasons. When Reverend Hammond begs him to forget the earthly world and pray for deliverance in the next world, Bigger imagines the preacher's religion as "a vast black silent void" (263). Ironically, Bigger at this precise moment of his life feels the need for light rather than darkness, and self-actualization rather than self-abnegation.

Conventional religious imagery is repeatedly undercut by irony throughout the novel. When Mrs. Dalton enters Mary's bedroom and discovers that her daughter has been drinking, she instinctively prays over Mary so that Mary will mend her ways, little realizing that her daughter is quite dead. When Bigger holds a hatchet over Mary's head before decapitating her, he is described as "pausing in an attitude of prayer" (91). While his outward posture might suggest sorrow over what he has done and even a desire to seek mercy, his inward thoughts, ironically, reveal only his grisly desire to cut off Mary's head so that he can fit her corpse into the furnace. Mr. Dalton is later perceived by Bigger as an omniscient "god" (164), but the ironic fact is that he is as blind and powerless as Bigger before a social system he can neither understand nor control.

Some readers have seen Bigger as a Christ figure who is "crucified" by white society and then achieves a kind of religious "salvation" by the end of the novel. But it is difficult to support this interpretation with a close reading of the novel. Unlike such books as Ken Kesey's *One Flew over the Cuckoo's Nest,* William Faulkner's *Light in August,* and Ignazio Silone's *Bread and Wine,* which tell the hero's story against a sustained pattern of allusions to Christ, *Native Son* makes but few explicit references to Christ's narrative when telling Bigger's story. And the few allusions to Christ in the novel are strongly ironic. Bigger certainly is not interested in taking Reverend Hammond's advice: "Be like Jesus. Don't Resist" (265). On the contrary, Bigger attacks his attackers and rebels against his condition in a most un-Christ-like way. When he removes the small cross from the chain around his neck and angrily throws it at the white people tormenting him, he shouts, "I can die without a cross" (313). As they torment him further by reminding him that only God can help him now and he had better put his soul in order, he cries out, "I ain't got no soul" (314).

Then too, Bigger's death at the end of the novel takes place on a much more private level than the death of Christ. While Christ was motivated by a love of humankind, Bigger goes to his death instead with a renewed sense of self-awareness. Even though Bigger does acquire a broader sympathy for those around him, these sympathies extend only to those with whom he has had personal contact. When Max asks him, "Do you love your people?" Bigger's reply is simply, "I don't know, Mr. Max" (330). And Wright certainly does not depict Bigger's death in messianic terms, as something that will regenerate the world. Unlike Christ, whose death created the possibility of salvation for humankind, Bigger dies "alone" (380) and his death leaves society and history unchanged. Bigger's story, when seen against the background of Christian narrative, therefore produces irony because its meanings jar so violently against the meanings of Christ's story.

Another broad pattern of ironic inversion in *Native Son* is the way it subverts the meanings of the Horatio Alger novels. As Michel Fabre has pointed out, Wright as a young man was "an avid reader of Horatio Alger" and believed deeply in "the myth of the self-made man, in the great American dream whereby everyone had an equal chance."[29] As an adult he came to see how the Alger myth was little more than a cruel joke for black people, since the doors of American opportunity were systematically closed to blacks because of their skin color. *Native Son* is therefore a conscious parody of the Alger novels, reducing to absurdity Alger's vision of America as an open society in which poor boys could go from "rags to riches" through good character, hard work, a little luck, and the support of a benevolent rich man. Boiled down to their simplest terms, all Alger novels repeat the same formula: A young orphan boy works his way from poverty to middle-class security by working hard at various menial jobs, educating himself at night, and performing heroic acts that eventually impress a gentleman who becomes his "sponsor." The typical Alger novel ends with the young boy proving his moral purity by altruistically performing an act that saves the life of a rich man's daughter. He is rewarded for his bravery in two ways: (1) In the short run, he is given a job in the rich man's business and is thus provided with an opportunity to work his way up the ladder of success, and (2) in the long run, he will marry the boss's daughter, securing his emotional happiness as well as his financial prosperity.

The Alger novels can be seen as secularized conversion narratives, in that they portray a dramatic transformation of a person from a penniless social outcast to a respectable citizen with unlimited possibilities. But the hero's "new life" is not generated by a mystical experience centered in Christ; rather, it is brought about by purely secular means, the hero's good character expressing itself in worldly acts of "service." The decisive force in such a process is not God's grace but a gentleman's goodwill. And the sign of conversion is not an inward sense of well-being but the accumulation of outward wealth and status.

Like Dreiser and Fitzgerald, Wright was fascinated with the Alger stories, seeing them as the expression of a fundamental American myth. *Native Son,* like *An American Tragedy* and *The Great Gatsby,* generates many of its most powerful meanings by consciously echoing and then ironically inverting the conventions of the Alger myth. To begin with, Bigger Thomas is like Alger's young hero in that he is at the bottom of American society and feels radically alone. Although he is not literally an orphan, he has lost his father in a race riot and has seen what is left of his family destroyed by the economic, social, and psychological pressures of American life. Like the Alger hero, Bigger wants to "rise" in American life, and he thinks he might be able to do this by coming to know a rich white man who will unlock the doors of American capitalism and show him the way to wealth. Coming out of the movie theater with Gus after they have watched a film about rich white people, Bigger is suddenly "filled with a sense of excitement about his new job" (35) because he feels that such a job will put him in contact with people who know the system and can teach him how to advance in it:

> Those were smart people; they knew how to get hold of money, millions of it. Maybe if he were working for them something would happen and he would get some of it. He would see just how they did it. Sure it was all a game and white people knew how to play it. And

rich white people were not so hard on Negroes; it was the poor whites who hated Negroes. . . . It was the rich white people who were smart and knew how to treat people. He remembered hearing somebody tell a story of a Negro chauffeur who had married a rich white girl and the girl's family had shipped them out of the country and had supplied them with money. (36)

Bigger's job as chauffeur therefore puts him precisely at the point where Alger's orphan boy is when he sells newspapers to rich men or shines their shoes. Although the job is menial, it locates him at the exact spot where poor and rich meet, thereby inspiring dreams of rising from a condition of poverty and magically entering the world of the rich. In its most romantic form, Bigger's dreams of success consist of marrying a "rich white girl" whose parents will transport him to a world of wealth and security. Bigger now sees rich white people as sponsors in a rags-to-riches novel, "smart," powerful people who can teach him to play the "game" of American success. Unlike poor whites, whose lowly status puts them in economic competition with blacks, rich whites are envisioned as benevolent mentors interested in helping deserving black people. Bigger's romantic vision of rich whites seems confirmed in his first meeting with the Daltons, when he discovers that they are liberal people who are well disposed toward blacks, have given large amounts of money to Negro education, and have also helped their previous chauffeur ascend the ladder of American success by sending him to evening school.

A closer look at the Daltons, however, reveals that they are quite different from the sponsors appearing in Alger novels and that Bigger ought to be very careful in his dealings with them. (As the novel turns out, he would have been better off had he obeyed his gut instincts and avoided them altogether.) Unlike Alger's gentlemen, who are moral guardians of the American system and oversee that system in an almost godly, omniscient way, the Daltons are "tragically blind" (362) and are therefore unable to help Bigger in his search for a better life.

First, they are blind to their own motives. Considering themselves to be philanthropists who unselfishly improve the lives of poverty-stricken blacks, they are unaware that they are instead driven by guilt stemming from the fact that their wealth is created by renting over-priced, substandard housing to blacks. Second, Mr. Dalton is blind to the nature of the economic and social system in which he participates. Although he consciously believes that hard work and good character enable a person to be a success in American life, he has made his fortune not by demonstrating good character but by exploiting ghetto blacks. When Max tries to make him see the connection between his wealth and the suffering of black people, he refuses to acknowledge this link, blindly declaring, "What do you want me to do? . . . Do you want me to die and atone for a suffering I never caused? I'm not responsible for the state of the world. I'm doing all one man can. I suppose you want me to take my money and fling it out to the millions who have nothing?" (274).

What Mr. Dalton fails to see is that he is *not* doing all he can to make America the open society it is portrayed to be in the Alger novels. By making his wealth from the systematic exploitation of black people and by not doing "something of a more fundamental nature" (274) to change the system, Mr. Dalton is closing, not opening, doors to people like Bigger Thomas. Mr. Dalton's "cold" question to Max implies that he lacks the human warmth truly to understand how he has caused much of the suffering he says he wants to alleviate. Rather than being a kindly sponsor to Bigger, Mr. Dalton is therefore one of Bigger's oppressors.

Similarly, Mary Dalton is an ironic inversion of the boss's daughter typically portrayed in the Alger books. Whereas Alger idealizes such figures as paragons of moral purity, Wright depicts Mary as sexually promiscuous and a heavy drinker. Whereas Alger sees the hero's marriage to the boss's daughter as a reward for the hero's own virtue, ensuring his entrance into a stable, fruitful, middle-class world, Wright makes it clear that Bigger and Mary could never marry, because a racist society forbids such unions. Despite the impressions he has received in movies and from apocryphal stories of chauffeurs marrying rich white girls, Bigger is barred from forming any kind of human relationship with Mary. As Max tells the court, American society has made people like Bigger and Mary strangers to each other. While they might occasionally engage in casual and secret sex, they could never develop a sustained and loving relationship, because society regards such relationships as the ultimate taboo. The final reward in Alger's novels is therefore forbidden to Bigger—he can never have the money, power, and status that Mary has by birth, and he can never "marry into" the comfortable world that Mary takes for granted. Ironically, his contact with Mary results not in expanded possibilities and a new life for Bigger but in his death.

That Bigger senses all this on a deeply subconcious level explains why his actual treatment of the Daltons is such a grim parody of how the typical Alger hero responds to his sponsors. Whereas Alger's orphan boy has a childlike trust in the rich gentleman who eventually becomes a father surrogate for him, Bigger is instinctively suspicious of the Daltons from the start and actually brings his gun with him on the day he reports to work. Whereas Alger's hero is eager to perform selfless acts of "service" to others in order to prove his moral worth to his sponsor, Bigger engages in criminal activity, trying to extort money from a rich man who represents an amoral system from which Bigger feels excluded. In a supremely ironic inversion of the central act of the Alger myth, Bigger does not fall in love with and marry the boss's daughter but instead kills her, decapitates her, and incinerates her in a furnace.

Wright's startling reversal of the Alger myth vividly emphasizes two main points. First, Wright clearly stresses that American capitalism does not work for blacks and other minorities. Such a system oppresses poor people on a daily basis, regardless of their good character or capacity for hard work. At best, American capitalism can make token gestures, for example, when the Daltons patronize their chauffeur by sending him to night school but then refuse to hire him in their business after he has graduated. Second, Wright emphasizes that blacks and other minorities must overturn American capitalism, pushing for radical changes that will ensure they become the "native sons" who fully share in the democratic possibilities of American life. Because the present system is rotten and corrupts people on all levels of society, from poor boys to rich sponsors, it must be replaced by a new system. As Max tells Mr. Dalton, "Something of a more fundamental nature must be done" (274) to make America the just and open society envisioned by the Founding Fathers and sentimentalized in the Alger books.

In "How Bigger Was Born" Wright observed that in writing *Native Son* he did not want to write a piece of fiction like his first book, *Uncle Tom's Children,* that could be mistaken for a sentimental story that would blur his reader's perceptions with tears: "I had written a book of short stories which was published under the title *Uncle Tom's Children.* When the reviews of that book began to appear, I realized I had made an awfully naive mistake. I found that I had written a book which even banker's daughters could read and weep over and feel good about. I swore to myself that if I ever wrote another book, no one would weep over it; that it would be so hard and deep that they would have to face it without the consolation of tears" (xxvii).

Native Son's consistently ironic tone produces a "hard and deep" book that results in a lucid awareness of American reality rather than a sentimental outlook that gives the reader the "consolation of tears." It is essential to realize, however, that Wright's ironies are not so bitter and reductive that they make *Native Son* a bleakly nihilistic book that cancels out all human meaning to Bigger's experience. Wright manages to make important affirmations after his novel's corrosive ironies have dissolved what is false in American life. Even though conventional religious values are ironically undercut throughout the novel, Wright stresses that Bigger does have a need for "certainty and faith" (109) and that he has a powerful spiritual yearning to find "a center, a core, an axis" (238) to his life. As we have seen in previous chapters, he finally discovers a center to his life when he develops an existential "faith" in himself. Even though Wright strips this faith of standard religious meanings and surrounds it with the irony that the state will execute Bigger shortly after he has fashioned a human identity for himself, Wright does indeed celebrate the psychological "conversion" that Bigger achieves.

Even Wright's handling of the Alger myth is not ultimately pessimistic. After he has used irony to demolish the sentimental clichés of the

Alger novels, he makes one more twist of irony to establish Bigger as a kind of "success story" after all. Just as Alger's hero achieves selfhood in his attempts to educate himself so that he can go from a condition of illiteracy to an ability to read and write, Bigger finally becomes a new kind of self-made man who has educated himself to the realities of American life and his own human nature. He clearly rejects the sort of formal education that Mr. Dalton proposes when he offers to send Bigger to night school, because Bigger realizes that such an education will enclose him in the impenetrable "night" that has blinded Dalton. Nevertheless, Bigger does informally educate himself by closely examining his own actions in the real world. This kind of self-education opens his eyes and enables him to undertake a decisive psychological journey. *Native Son* therefore subverts the conventions of the Alger myth in order to redefine that myth, ultimately positing a new kind of psychological and moral "success" for its hero.

Unlike fundamentally pessimistic works—such as Jean-Paul Sartre's *Nausea,* Samuel Beckett's *Happy Days,* and Louis-Ferdinand Céline's *Journey to the End of Night*—that employ massive patterns of irony to undercut all human meanings and thus envision modern experience as a colossal void, *Native Son* uses irony both to attack false values and to create new values in their place. As a result, Wright's masterwork possesses a thematic complexity missing in many modern books, especially those arising from existential and naturalistic traditions.

10

Theme

When discussing the central ideas, or themes, in *Native Son,* it is important to realize they do not come to us in abstract form, as do the ideas in a discursive or analytical essay. While the essayist's job is to abstract ideas from human experience and then articulate these ideas clearly and efficiently, the novelist's task is to embody ideas—that is, to present them as part of a whole dramatic experience that is unfolding before the reader's eyes. As the Russian writer Nickolai Gogol once said, "My business is to speak with living images and not with arguments. I must present life as it is and not write essays about it."[30] Joseph Conrad, a novelist whom Wright very much admired, made a similar point when he said, "My task is by the power of the written word, to make you hear, to make you feel it is, before all, to make you *see!*"[31] In the same way, Wright saw fiction as a dramatic re-creation of whole experiences rather than a reduction of experience to the level of simple ideas. As he said in "How Bigger Was Born," he wanted to "render" and "depict" (xxxi) Bigger's life and not merely summarize it or abstractly analyze it.

Native Son in many ways is a novel of ideas, but these ideas do not come to us as a simplified thesis proving a narrowly propagandistic point. Rather, they are presented as complex themes embedded in a richly imagined, multidimensional experience. The various aspects of the novel's form constitute an organic unity that helps Wright to recreate human experience on many levels. The setting establishes a physically substantial world that strongly arouses all the readers' senses, especially sight and sound. As we have seen, the setting also has emotional value, for it is often used brilliantly as a reflector of Bigger's deepest feelings. The novel's structure also enriches the novel's themes as they emerge from intricate patterns of image and action that make simple ideas reverberate against one another, thus creating richer, more nuanced ideas that are also rooted in Bigger's specific experiences. Characterization likewise forces us to perceive the novel's themes as they arise from the concrete experiences of the people who populate the novel. Point of view further personalizes and intensifies the novel's ideas by pushing them through the central character's unique consciousness. Finally, the novel's tone tinges all the book's ideas with complicated ironies that make it impossible for the reader to reduce the novel's meaning to simplistic statements.

All the literary techniques we have studied separately are skillfully integrated in a formal unity that creates a very rich experience for the reader. The reader must therefore be careful not to oversimplify that experience by pulling certain ideas out of the dense texture of the novel, thus converting its complicated themes to a simplified thesis. This caution applies especially when working with Wright's political themes. At the time he completed *Native Son,* Wright was still a member of the Communist party and he took very seriously certain ideas central to Marxist ideology. But he was also at a sensitive point in his own personal development, one where he had grown critical of certain aspects of communism and was becoming increasingly suspicious of ideology as something that could limit a writer's vision and inhibit his freedom of expression. *Native Son* reflects this tension powerfully, for it is both a seriously political novel and a deeply personal novel expressing reservations about politics in general and communism in particular.

It would therefore be a mistake to reduce the novel to a crude piece of propaganda centered in simplistic ideas about Marxist revolution. Although some early readers of the novel did precisely this, their readings distorted both Wright's intentions and the novel he wrote. Such critics saw American capitalism as the novel's villain and figures like Jan and Max as heroes because they offer a human alternative to capitalism in a Communist state that will develop after a proletarian revolution. According to this interpretation, Bigger emerges as a revolutionary martyr who is converted to the cause only to be executed by the state.

This essentially melodramatic interpretation does real violence to Wright's novel because it inserts highly simplified versions of Marxist ideology in place of the novel's actual themes. Throughout the novel, Wright is very much preoccupied with Marxist ideology, but his view of it is much more complicated than this oversimplified interpretation would allow. For example, Jan's enthusiastic but facile view of the coming revolution is clearly undercut by the narrator, who sees political reality in much more sophisticated terms than Jan does. Jan's naiveté is especially evident when he tries to communicate his Marxist view of the future as he and Bigger contemplate the Chicago skyline from a fast-moving automobile:

> "We'll own all that some day, Bigger," Jan said with a wave of his hand. "After the revolution it'll be ours. But we'll have to fight for it. What a world to win, Bigger! And when that day comes, things'll be different. There'll be no white and no black; there'll be no rich and no poor."
>
> Bigger said nothing. The car whirred along. (69)

Jan's ideas are part of a dramatic situation that surrounds these ideas with ironies, making us aware that Wright's political views are a good deal more tough-minded and complex than Jan's naive statements. First, Jan's declaration of solidarity with black people and poor people contrasts sharply with the concrete situation he is in, as he preaches such abstractions to a mute audience who feels quite distant from him. Despite Jan's verbal attempts to establish rapport with Bigger, who is indeed both poor and black, the result of his talk is to make Bigger feel uncomfortable with him at best and resentful of him at worst. Indeed, the more Jan talks about a revolution that will join black and white people together, the more Bigger recoils from him, for Bigger feels toward people like Jan "a dumb, cold, and inarticulate hate" (68) that political rhetoric is unlikely to dissolve. Jan's naive grasp of ideology has blinded him to the fact that many centuries of painful history have divided people into rich and poor, black and white, and that it will take more than talk to remove these differences. When Jan suggests that people will eventually have to go beyond talk and "fight" for revolution, his views are also undermined with irony. As Bigger's experience dramatically shows, violence can also be a bitter disappointment, promising liberation but often resulting in destruction.

Max's beliefs in Marxism and communism are not as naive as Jan's but also fall well short of the complex political themes at the center of the novel. Max is clearly not a spokesman for Wright's views, as some leftist critics have tried to argue, because his position in the novel is constantly weakened by ironies created by the dramatic situations in which he is placed. This point is suggested in Bigger's very first meeting with Max, wherein Max is presented in a somewhat sympathetic but also ironic way. His "quiet, firm, but kind" (269) voice puts Bigger at ease, and his offer to "help" (269) Bigger by representing him in court also impresses Bigger. But there are a few qualities about Max that bother both the reader and Bigger, even at this point. Bigger first perceives Max in mildly surrealistic terms: "He saw a man's head come into the door, a head strange and white" (269), a description reminiscent of the way he had earlier seen Mrs. Dalton as a white blur. The description suggests what is later confirmed, that Max is in some ways a disembodied "head" who is capable of grasping ideas in the abstract but who has trouble understanding people. And although Max is surely well disposed toward Bigger, his motives for representing him in court are more political than personal, for at the end of the scene Max tells Buckley, "If you had not dragged the name of the Communist Party into the murder, I'd not be here" (271). Max's very impersonal response to Bigger is also emphasized by the fact that he rarely addresses Bigger by name. He usually refers to him as "this boy," apparently unaware of the insulting connotations this phrase might have for a 20-year-old black male.

From the very beginning, then, one gets the strong impression that Max's "strange and white" head perceives Bigger from a considerable distance, filtering him through a set of ideas that Max understands much better than the particular person before him. This aspect is vividly dramatized in the way Max presents Bigger's case, since the whole thrust of his defense is to raise the court's political consciousness with a Marxist interpretation of history while doing very little for Bigger as an individual. Max premises his case on a plea for mercy, but much of what he says about Bigger reinforces the court's dim view of Bigger as a pathological figure rather than a person capable of rehabilitation. Oddly enough, Max bases his case on the misconception that Bigger "murdered" (363) Mary, and he uses this word many times to describe what we know is an accidental killing. His detailed description of Bigger's "murder" of Mary as "the most meaningful, exciting, and stirring thing that ever happened to him" (364) might convince his leftist colleagues of the brutalities of American capitalism but will do little to create mercy for Bigger in the hearts of the judge or the enraged mobs outside the courtroom. Max also does Bigger no good when he tells the court, "Every time he comes in contact with us he kills. . . . Every thought he thinks is a potential murder. . . . *His very existence is a crime against the state!*" (367). Although Max's ideas in the abstract have some validity, the concrete situation before him as Bigger's lawyer requires that he address the court in a shrewder, more restrained way.

It is therefore not surprising that Max and Bigger separate by the end of the novel. Although Bigger desperately wants to tell his personal story to Max and thus go to his death with the satisfaction that someone has finally understood him, Max is too blinded by abstraction to see Bigger in such personal terms. The novel does not end with a burst of propaganda by describing Max and Bigger arm in arm as they sing the "Internationale." Rather, it concludes with Max's vision blurred with tears as he turns his back to Bigger while walking down the corridor. When Bigger calls him in a final attempt to establish eye contact with Max, the narrator reveals that "Max [does] not turn around" (392) but instead leaves the novel uttering a weak good-bye.

James Baldwin notwithstanding, *Native Son* is not a "problem novel" centering on a social dilemma that is neatly resolved by a simplistic political thesis. Bigger's situation is too complex to be understood by the political abstractions that distort the vision of both Jan and Max. But it would be equally misleading to read the novel in an entirely personal way, interpreting its central themes as a categorical rejection of politics and a celebration of the isolated individual. Wright makes it clear that part of Bigger's personality has a deeply felt need to establish political bonds with other black people: "There were rare moments when a feeling and longing for solidarity with other black people would take hold of him. . . . As he rode, looking at the black people on the sidewalk, he felt that one way to end fear and shame was to make all those black people act together, rule them, tell them what to do, and make them do it. Dimly, he felt that there should be one direction in which he and all other black people could go wholeheartedly" (109). Later in the novel, Bigger's wish to establish unity with all black people broadens to a desire to establish kinship with all oppressed people. In this sense Jan and Max, although they do not solve his problems, are nevertheless important to him because they nourish Bigger's social self by suggesting that politics can be a way of meaningfully connecting the individual to other people. Partly because of his relationship with Jan and Max, Bigger can begin to overcome the severe alienation that has stunted his growth. Though Jan and Max are not elevated to the level of heroes in a political allegory, neither are they reduced to the status of the "wild and crazy . . . reds" (58) that Peggy has described to Bigger and that he also sees stereotyped in films and newspaper cartoons.

Wright's political themes, then, are not simplified ideas neatly abstracted from the dense texture of lived experience. *Native Son* is neither a crudely Marxist novel nor an equally simplistic antipolitical book. Instead, its themes are generated by the dialectical pull of opposite ideas as they interact with each other. Wright's final vision in

Native Son is like the complicated "double vision" toward which Bigger gropes in book Three: "He looked out upon the world and the people about him with a double vision, an image of him, alone, sitting strapped in the electric chair and waiting for the hot current to leap through his body; and the other vision pictured life, an image of himself standing amid throngs of men, lost in the welter of their lives with the hope of emerging again, different, unafraid" (337). Such a central theme forces us to see Bigger in both personal and political terms, for his identity is rooted both in his need to see himself in the context of "throngs of men" and in his equally compelling need to be "alone." He is therefore both a typical figure who, in Marxist terms, represents the dispossessed masses and also a fully particularized individual who, in existentialist terms, has an autonomous self.

The novel's thematic complexity can also be seen when we consider the much-discussed problem of its "naturalism." Many critics responding to this issue have oversimplified the novel's central theme, some contending that the book offers an absolutely deterministic vision of life and others arguing that the novel asserts that free will is finally stronger than environmental determinants. A careful reading of *Native Son* reveals, however, that the novel's main theme consists of a complex interplay of these two ideas, for Wright offers a vision of life in which man is both strongly conditioned by environment and able in certain ways to transform himself and his environment through consciousness and free will. As we have seen, Bigger is born into a restrictive environment and by the end of the novel his outward life is still determined by that environment, which has literally trapped him in a prison cell and will soon take his life. But he is no longer the complete victim of environment who cried out early in the novel that "something awful's going to happen to me. . . . It's like I was going to do something I can't help" (24). By the end of the novel, Bigger is in control of his inward life, and he can use this inward life to direct himself in the outer world. While it is true that he cannot change the fact that he is imprisoned and will soon be executed, he is psychologically liberated by the knowledge that he can meet his death in a controlled, dignified way after he has come to human terms with himself and others.

Theme

Reading *Native Son* is therefore a complicated but rewarding experience because its themes grow out of a rich enactment of life on many levels. Accordingly, readers in search of the "meaning" of *Native Son* should not look for a simple moral or a formulaic thesis that mechanically resolves the tension of ideas at the core of the novel. *Native Son* is not a thin essay "about" life; it is instead a powerful work of art that sets ideas in motion, thus re-creating the full weight and density of lived experience.

Conclusion

As many critics have rightly stressed, *Native Son* is a landmark novel that created important new directions in literature. But it is also a work deeply rooted in a number of interrelated literary traditions. Although Wright's formal schooling was limited, he was a voracious reader who had a solid understanding of modern, American, and Afro-American traditions. Part of the extraordinary resonance of *Native Son* can be explained by the way it naturally grows out of and extends these traditions.

From the beginning, Wright makes us aware of *Native Son* as a representative modern work whose hero exhibits strong kinship with such figures as Dostoyevski's marginal men, Zola's victims, and Ibsen's rebels, for Bigger, like most modern protagonists, is first perceived as a stranger who must confront a social world in which conventions and traditional values have broken down to a point where he feels a deep sense of alienation leading to an identity crisis. Wright's preface to *Native Son* described Bigger's uniquely modern situation as follows:

> But more than anything else, as a writer, I was fascinated by the similarity of the emotional tensions of Bigger in America and Bigger in Nazi Germany and Bigger in old Russia. All Bigger Thomases, white and black, felt tense, nervous, hysterical, restless. From far

Conclusion

away Nazi Germany and old Russia had come to me items of knowledge that told me that certain modern experiences were creating types of personalities whose existence ignored racial and national lines of demarcation, that these personalities carried with them a more universal drama element than anything I had ever encountered before; that these personalities were mainly imposed upon *men and women living in a world whose fundamental assumptions could no longer be taken for granted: a world ridden by national class strife; a world whose metaphysical meanings had vanished; a world in which God no longer existed as a daily focus of men's lives; a world in which men could no longer retain their faith in an ultimate hereafter.* (xix; my italics)

Modern America, like nineteenth-century Russia and 1930s Germany, was for Wright a culture in severe crisis, caught in a moment of history that called into sharp question all traditional values that in previous ages gave people a sense of identity. Because conventional religious and philosophical meanings could no longer be made consistent with the brutal facts of modern existence, Wright believed that "God no longer existed as a daily focus of men's lives" and modern people were forced to face "a world whose metaphysical meanings had vanished." A direct consequence of this collapse of traditional values was a corresponding breakdown of the social conventions and institutions that had rested upon those values. The complete dissolution of czarist Russia and the political chaos of Germany after World War I offered Wright compelling models of what happens to society when traditional assumptions no longer square with the hard facts of history. He saw a similar breakdown in American culture during the Great Depression, a world poised dangerously on the edge of economic collapse and world war.

Given this dissolution of old faiths and a weakening of the established social order, Wright believed that "new types of personalities" emerge in literature and history. Such people can no longer work out human identities by connecting themselves to stable frames of reference outside the self, such as conventional social values or traditional religion; they must therefore face the void of modern life. Deeply alienated from external reality, modern man must either succumb to a meaningless world as a passive antihero or attempt to achieve heroic status by either discovering new sources of meaning or revitalizing old ones.

Bigger Thomas finds himself in this uniquely modern situation. Everywhere around him he sees the absence of meaning, as traditional sources of value have eroded and no new values have emerged to replace them. Like Ibsen's Nora Helmer, Bigger views society as a threat to his identity because its institutions and values stifle him with roles that cancel out his most human impulses. Just as Nora rejects a sexist society because it suffocates her with the roles of mother and wife, which are at variance with the promptings of her real self, so too does Bigger reject a racist society because he feels demeaned by the limited roles it makes available to him. While he aspires literally and figuratively to the role of "aviator" (327) because it satisfies his urges for freedom, mobility, and control, society forces him into the role of chauffeur, making him an extension of the will of others. Like many other modern figures—for example, Flaubert's Emma Bovary and Sartre's Roquentin—Bigger finds that things only get worse when he looks toward conventional religion. Although he has a deep need for "certainty and faith" (109), the forms of religion available to him have been degraded to the point where they can offer him only cheap illusion rather than genuine belief. He scorns the fundamentalist religion of his mother and Reverend Hammond because he feels it has produced spiritual impoverishment, resulting in their acceptance of dehumanized roles of submissive Negroes. Even when Bigger looks toward secular equivalents to religion, such as the worship of success preached by people like the Daltons, he feels betrayed, for such a "church" does not open its doors to blacks. Ultimately, the American belief in outward success is just as blinding as his mother's version of Christianity.

Rather than accept such a bleak world and his meaningless position in it, Bigger attempts to discover fresh meanings to life that can lead to the establishment of a human identity. Like Dostoyevski's Raskolnikov, he is deeply shaken by the violence of his own criminal activity, and this feeling results in a reawakening of his conscience and a deepening of his consciousness. Although he cannot ground his life, as does Raskolnikov, in a revitalized belief in traditional religion, he can commit himself to "a new hope" (256) in other sources of meaning. Part of this meaning comes through Max's political vision, which stresses Bigger's kinship with all oppressed people. While Bigger never becomes "converted" to either Marxism or communism, he nevertheless learns from Max that perhaps there is an alternative to the dehumanizing capitalistic society that has victimized him.

Although not an intellectual, Bigger also achieves what Flaubert called the "heroism of the mind"[32] by journeying deeply within himself. Like Dostoyevski's underground man and Camus's Meursault, he can create meaning in an otherwise absurd world by unlocking the doors to his consciousness, even while trapped in an outward prison. This deepening of consciousness enables Bigger to take responsibility for his actions and to become, within certain limits, a freely willing director of his own life rather than a passive receptor of environmental stimuli.

Native Son, however, is not only an integral part of European modernism; it is also deeply rooted in a specifically American tradition. Wright read widely in classic American literature and was especially influenced by Poe, Hawthorne, and James. He was also strongly influenced by such modern American novelists as Dreiser, Anderson, and Farrell. Wright, who once observed that "the Negro is America's metaphor,"[33] fully intended that *Native Son* would reverberate meaningfully in American literary tradition and titled his novel to suggest that his central character was a representative American figure. To further stress the specifically American qualities of his work, he consciously echoed American masterpieces at crucial points in *Native Son*. As several critics have pointed out, the white cat that terrifies Bigger is a cleverly ironic version of the black cat that terrifies Poe's villain in "The Black Cat." Bigger's fascination with the fiery furnace in the Daltons' basement reminds us not only of Ishmael's fascination with the tryworks in *Moby-Dick* but also of Ethan Brand's compulsion to examine the fires of the limekiln in Hawthorne's story. At one point in *Native Son* Wright also ironically echoes Benjamin Franklin's famous entry into Philadelphia. Like Franklin, who uses his last pennies to buy bread, which he then tucks under his arm as he brashly walks through the city in search of a new life, Bigger will use his last 7¢ to buy a loaf of bread, which he also puts under his arm while he walks through the South Side of Chicago in an attempt to escape the police. But whereas the mythical image of Franklin establishes him as a poor boy on the rise, the naturalistic image of Bigger portrays him as a victim of an environment that will soon imprison him.

What makes *Native Son* most American, however, is its conception of the hero. Bigger resembles classic American heroes like Natty Bumppo and Huckleberry Finn because he is essentially a loner who is lightly tied to family, and he rebels against society because it deprives him of the freedom and independence he desires. Like the typical American picaresque hero, his deepest longings are revealed when he contemplates images of open space and free movement. Although deprived of the romantic forms of free space—such as Ishmael's seas, Whitman's open road, and Huck Finn's territories—Bigger can nevertheless feel the American picaresque hero's urge for radical forms of freedom when he observes a plane flying by or when he drives Mr. Dalton's powerful automobile. Even though Bigger remains physically confined throughout the novel, he does undergo an important psychological journey, one in which he follows "a strange path into a strange land" (107) of the inward self. He thus takes "a new path" (142) in life and eventually finds a "road" leading him to "a sure and quiet knowledge"(226) of himself and his world, for late in the novel he is portrayed as "groping forward with fierce zeal" (288) to a deeper knowledge of self. Like Dreiser's Carrie Meeber and other American picaros, Bigger is frustrated by his movements in external reality but can move significantly through his own inner space.

This deeply psychological focus of *Native Son* also links it strongly to the gothic tradition in American fiction. The world as seen through Bigger's mind is a continuous nightmare filled with rats, "ghosts," eerie cats, rotting buildings that resemble skulls, and city streets that are strange labyrinths leading nowhere. Such a world triggers in the hero the same kind of fear that suffuses Poe's fiction and the same kind of guilt that pulses through Hawthorne's stories. Like Melville, Wright was shocked by his recognition of the dark underside of American life and was not fooled by its bright but shallow optimism.

Lastly, *Native Son* is vitally connected to Afro-American folk tradition, especially as that tradition manifests itself in oral tales, the blues, spirituals, and sermons. In an essay entitled "The Literature of the Negro in the United States," Wright described his own roots in this folk tradition and stressed its importance for modern Afro-American literature: "Because I feel personally identified with the migrant Negro, his folk songs, his ditties, his wild tales of bad men; and because my own life was forged in the depths in which they live, I'll tell first of [them]. Numerically this formless folk utterance accounts for the great majority of the Negro people in the United States, and it is my conviction that the subject matter of future novels and poems resides in the lives of these nameless millions" (*White Man,* 85–86). As several critics have pointed out, Bigger Thomas closely resembles the heroes of black folk stories, particularly "badmen" like Stackolee and tricksters like Brer Rabbit. *Native Son* also crackles with the sharp ironies of blues music, a musical tradition Wright studied carefully and even participated in when he wrote some blues songs early in his career.

Moreover, Wright's masterwork makes skillful use of black religious expression, employing imagery from the sermons and spirituals to communicate dramatically new meanings. In *Black Boy* Wright notes that however much he recoiled from the literal implications of the fire-and-brimstone religion his grandmother tried to impose on him, he was aesthetically drawn to its compelling symbolism and apocalyptic sense of life: "Many of the religious symbols appealed to my sensibilities and I responded to the dramatic vision of life held by the church, feeling that to live day by day with death as one's sole thought was to be so compassionately sensitive toward all life as to view all men as slowly dying, and the trembling sense of fate that welled up, sweet and melancholy, from the hymns blended with the sense of fate that I had already caught from life" (*BB,* 123–24). The church's "dramatic vision of life" stirred Wright deeply, since it embedded in him a fateful sense of death that made him "compassionately sensitive toward all life." Like Bigger Thomas, whose consciousness is quickened by his impending death, Wright scrutinized life with special care partly because of the ominous sense of death he received from his grandmother's fundamentalist religion. The church's dramatic vision of life also stirred Wright deeply in another important way, for it provided him with many archetypal images that he used brilliantly in his fiction, particularly in *Native Son*. Fire, which Keneth Kinnamon has recently described as "a central metaphor of [Wright's] creative imagination,"[34] is used throughout the novel to dramatize some of Bigger's deepest emotions. Dramatic images of light and darkness, which Wright also derived from the fundamentalist religion he was exposed to as a young man, are also used extensively. Most of the key scenes of violence are acted out in darkness to suggest the environmental pressures that blind Bigger and force him to act in a compulsively brutal way. But Bigger's human growth by the end of the novel is signaled by his conscious movement toward "light." At the inquest, for example, he resolves not to act "blindly" but feels "he would have to have light in order to act now" (289). Taking such striking images from a religious background whose dogma and institutional life he could never accept, Wright transformed such imagery to express important psychological meanings.

Thus drinking from a rich variety of cultural streams, all of which flow in a deep and complex harmony, *Native Son* is a major achievement in modern literature. Wright's novel not only revitalized modern, American, and Afro-American traditions by creating a new kind of hero and providing a fresh look at black urban life but also deepened its own meanings by connecting the hero's experience to these multiple levels of literary tradition. It therefore achieved the originality, depth, and resonance expected of a genuine masterwork.

Notes and References

1. August Meir and Elliott Rudwick, *From Plantation to Ghetto,* (New York: Hill & Wang, 1970), 213.

2. John Hope Franklin, *From Slavery to Freedom: A History of Negro Americans,* 3d. Ed. (New York: Knopf, 1967), 482.

3. "I Tried to Be a Communist," in *The God That Failed,* ed. Richard Crossman (New York: Bantam Books, 1952), 105, 117, 141.

4. *American Hunger* (New York: Harper & Row, 1977), 119.

5. Alfred Kazin, *On Native Grounds* (Garden City, N.Y.: Doubleday, 1956), 283–84.

6. Irving Howe, "Black Boys and *Native Sons,*" in *Twentieth Century Interpretations of Native Son,* ed. Houston Baker (Englewood Cliffs, N.J.: Prentice Hall, 1972), 63; hereafter cited in the text.

7. James Weldon Johnson, *The Autobiography of An Ex-Colored Man,* in *Three Negro Classics,* ed. John Hope Franklin (New York: Avon Books, 1965), 441, 435.

8. Robert Bone, *The Negro Novel in America* (New Haven, Conn.: Yale University Press, 1958), 157.

9. Clarence Major, "Necessary Distance: Afterthoughts on Becoming a Writer," *Black American Literature Forum* 23 (Summer 1989); 220.

10. Keneth Kinnamon, *The Emergence of Richard Wright: A Study in Literature and Society* (Urbana: University of Illinois Press, 1972), 118; hereafter cited in the text.

11. William Gardner Smith, "The Negro Writer: Pitfalls and Compensations," *Phylon* 11 (Fourth Quarter 1950); 298.

12. Hugh Gloster, *Negro Voices in American Fiction* (Chapel Hill: University of North Carolina Press, 1948), 233–34.

13. James Baldwin, *Notes of a Native Son* (Boston: Beacon Press, 1955) 41, 34.

14. Eldridge Cleaver, *Soul on Ice* (New York: Dell, 1968), 108–9, 106.

15. George E. Kent, "Richard Wright: Blackness and the Adventures of Western Culture," *CLA Journal* 12 (June 1969): 340; hereafter cited in the text.

16. Donald B. Gibson, "Wright's Invisible *Native Son*," *American Quarterly* 21, no. 4 (Winter 1969): 731; hereafter cited in the text.

17. Dan McCall, *The Example of Richard Wright* (New York: Harcourt, Brace, and World, 1969), 77.

18. Blyden Jackson, "Richard Wright: Black Boy from America's Black Belt and Urban Ghettos: *CLA Journal* 12 (June 1969): 289, 309.

19. Robert Felgar, *Richard Wright* (Boston: Twayne Publishers, 1980), 9, 108.

20. Jerry Bryant, "The Violence of *Native Son*," *Southern Review* 17 (April 1981): 305.

21. Michael G. Cooke, *Afro-American Literature in the Twentieth Century: The Achievement of Intimacy* (New Haven, Conn.: Yale University Press, 1984), 88, 96–97.

22. Calvin Hernton, "The Sexual Mountain and Black Women Writers," *Black American Literature Forum* 18 (Winter 1984): 139.

23. Barbara Johnson, "The Re(a)d and the Black," in *Richard Wright's Native Son,* ed. Harold Bloom (New York: Chelsea House, 1988), 120.

24. Maria K. Mootry, "Bitches, Whores, and Woman Haters: Archetypes and Typologies in the Art of Richard Wright,"in *Richard Wright: A Collection of Critical Essays,* ed. Richard Macksey and Frank E. Moorer (Englewood Cliffs, N.J.: Prentice Hall, 1984), 127, 123, 127.

25. Houston Baker, *Long Black Song* (Charlottesville: University of Virginia Press, 1972), 127.

26. Foreword to *The Meaning of the Blues,* by Paul Oliver (New York: Collier Books, 1960), 9.

27. Ralph Ellison, *Shadow and Act* (New York: New American Library, 1966), 104.

28. Ross Pudaloff, "Celebrity as Identity: Richard Wright, *Native Son,* and Mass Culture," *Studies in American Fiction* 11 (Spring 1983): 4.

29. Michel Fabre, *The Unfinished Quest of Richard Wright,* trans. Isabel Barzun (New York: Morrow, 1973), 51.

30. Nickolai Gogol, *The Overcoat and Other Tales of Good and Evil,* trans. David Magarshack (New York: Norton, 1957), 10.

31. Joseph Conrad, "Preface to *The Nigger of the Narcissus,*" in *Joseph Conrad: Tales of Land and Sea* (Garden City, N.Y.: Hanover House, 1953), 107.

32. Gustave Flaubert, *Correspondance,* in *Oeuvres Complètes* (Paris: Conrad, 1926), 456; my translation.

33. *White Man, Listen!* (Garden City, N.Y.: Doubleday, 1964), 72; hereafter cited in the text.

34. Keneth Kinnamon, *New Essays on Native Son* (Cambridge, England: Cambridge University Press, 1990), 15.

Selected Bibliography

Primary Works

Fiction
Uncle Tom's Children. New York: Harper & Brothers, 1938.
Native Son. New York: Harper & Brothers, 1940.
The Outsider. New York: Harper & Brothers, 1953.
Savage Holiday. New York: Avon Books, 1954.
The Long Dream. New York: Doubleday, 1958.
Eight Men. Cleveland: World, 1961.
Lawd Today. New York: Avon Books, 1963.

Nonfiction
"Blueprint for Negro Writing." *New Challenge* 2 (Fall 1937): 53–65. Wright urges black writers to abandon literary strategies accomodating them to the expectations of white America and to develop a mode of writing whose vision is Marxist and nationalist.

"The Ethics of Living Jim Crow." *American Stuff: A WPA Writers Anthology.* New York: Viking Press (1937): 39–52. Wright's depiction of his southern experiences, reprinted in a number of anthologies, including *Black Voices,* edited by Abraham Chapman (New York: New American Library, 1968, 288–98).

"How Bigger Was Born" (pamphlet). New York: Harper & Brothers, 1940. Wright's account of the composition of *Native Son* and its roots in his own experiences; the pamphlet is widely reprinted and appears as the introduction to the Perennial Classics paperback edition of the novel (New York: Harper & Row, 1966).

Twelve Million Black Voices. New York: Viking Press, 1941.

Selected Bibliography

"I Tried to Be a Communist" *Atlantic Monthly,* August 1944, 61–70. Wright's account of his disaffection with the Communist party; the article is included in *The God That Failed,* edited by Richard Crossman (New York: Bantam Books, 1952).

Black Boy. New York: Harper & Brothers, 1945.

Black Power. New York: Harper & Brothers, 1954.

The Color Curtain. Cleveland: World, 1954.

Pagan Spain. New York: Harper & Row, 1957.

White Man, Listen! New York: Doubleday, 1957.

American Hunger. New York: Harper & Row, 1977. Wright's account of his years in Chicago, some of which was published posthumously.

Secondary Works

Bibliographies

Fabre, Michel, and Charles T. Davis. *Richard Wright: A Primary Bibliography.* Boston: G. K. Hall, 1982. A bibliography of Wright's published and unpublished works, with annotations.

Kinnamon, Keneth (with the help of Joseph Benson, Michel Fabre, and Craig Werner). *A Richard Wright Bibliography: Fifty Years of Criticism and Commentary, 1933–1982.* Westport, Conn.: Greenwood Press, 1988. A monumental and indispensable bibliographic study, examining 50 years of secondary sources, including books, journal articles, newspaper and scholarly reviews, doctoral dissertations, master's theses, encyclopedia entries, handbooks, study guides, interviews, published letters, and chapters in books. Annotations are usually brief but at times well detailed.

Reilly, John. "Richard Wright: An Essay in Bibliography." *Resources for American Literary Study* (Autumn 1971): 131–80. An incisive, carefully detailed survey of Wright scholarship from its beginnings to 1970.

Books

Brignano, Russell. *Richard Wright: An Introduction to His Works.* Pittsburgh: University of Pittsburgh Press, 1970. An early study that surveys central themes in Wright's fiction in light of the main developments of his life. It lays heavy stress on his existentialism, playing down his role in the Communist party.

Fabre, Michel. *The Unfinished Quest of Richard Wright,* translated by Isabel Barzun. New York: Morrow, 1973. The best literary biography of

Wright, examining Wright's experience without being restricted by a narrow thesis. Chapters on Wright's growing up in the South and his expatriate days are particularly good.

Felgar, Robert. *Richard Wright.* Boston: Twayne Publishers, 1980. A general survey of Wright's life and career. *Native Son* is read in light of Eldridge Cleaver's theories of sex and race.

Gayle, Addison. *Richard Wright: Ordeal of a Native Son.* New York: Doubleday, 1980. A "political" biography that uses information about Wright that Gayle obtained under the Freedom of Information Act. From the information he got from files the FBI kept on Wright, Gayle concludes that Wright was harassed by government agencies intent on discrediting his criticism of U.S. foreign policy and that this harassment may have played a role in his premature death.

Joyce, Joyce Ann. *Richard Wright's Art of Tragedy.* Iowa City: University of Iowa Press, 1986. A brief but revealing study of Wright's craftsmanship, arguing that Bigger Thomas is a tragic hero, not a naturalistic victim.

Kinnamon, Keneth. *The Emergence of Richard Wright: A Study in Literature and Society.* Urbana: University of Illinois Press, 1972. A study of Wright's life, literary career, and social milieu, from his birth in 1908 to the publication of *Native Son* in 1940. An essential book for all Wright scholars.

McCall, Dan. *The Example of Richard Wright.* New York: Harcourt, Brace and World, 1969. A penetrating analysis of Bigger and a sensitive discussion of Wright as a surrealistic writer.

Margolies, Edward. *The Art of Richard Wright.* Carbondale: Southern Illinois University Press, 1969. A study of Wright's life and art, arguing that *Native Son* centers on three kinds of revolutions: communism, existentialism, and black nationalism.

Reilly, John. *Richard Wright: The Critical Reception.* New York: Franklin, 1978. An indispensable collection of early reviews of Wright's major works. Its introductions provide a clear survey of patterns in Wright scholarship as well as valuable historical background.

Webb, Constance. *Richard Wright: A Biography.* New York: Putnam, 1968. An early biography written by a close friend of Wright's.

Chapters in Books

Baker, Houston. *Long Black Song: Essays in Black American Literature.* Charlottesville: University Press of Virginia, 1972. Baker praises *Native Son* for being the first novel to capture the full scope and force of black folklore.

Baldwin, James. *Notes of a Native Son.* Boston: Beacon Press, 1955. "Everybody's Protest Novel" and "Many Thousands Gone" submit *Native Son* to serious criticism, alleging that the novel fails because its propagandistic intent destroys its artistic integrity. Baldwin sees Bigger Thomas as a stereotypical "monster" and chides Wright for drawing an excessively bleak, deterministic vision of black life.

————. *Nobody Knows My Name: More Notes of a Native Son.* New York: Dell, 1961. Although still critical of Wright, Baldwin here offers a more generous assessment of Wright's work than appeared in *Notes of a Native Son.* Summing up Wright's work a year after his death, Baldwin claims that "Wright's unrelentingly bleak landscape was not merely that of the Deep South, or of Chicago, but that of the world, the human heart."

Bell, Bernard. *The Afro-American Novel and Its Tradition.* Amherst: University of Massachusetts Press, 1987. A reappraisal of *Native Son* that criticizes the novel on cultural and artistic grounds.

Bone, Robert. *The Negro Novel in America.* New Haven, Conn.: Yale University Press, 1958. Bone praises *Native Son* for its strong influence on black literature but criticizes it as a work of art.

Cleaver, Eldridge. *Soul on Ice.* New York: Dell, 1968. Cleaver angrily responds to Baldwin's criticism of *Native Son,* defending the novel for its social vision and political militancy.

Cooke, Michael. *Afro-American Literature in the Twentieth Century: The Achievement of Intimacy.* New Haven, Conn.: Yale University Press, 1984. Cooke maintains that Bigger's growth involves a movement from masking the self to boldly asserting the self. At his death, he is on the verge of "intimacy," connecting the self with the world.

Davis, Arthur P. *From the Dark Tower: Afro-American Writers, 1900 to 1960.* Washington, D.C.: Howard University Press, 1974. Davis argues that *Native Son* represents the culmination of Wright's powers as a writer; all his early work moves steadily to "the heights" of *Native Son,* and his subsequent work is a gradual decline from it.

Ellison, Ralph. *Shadow and Act.* New York: Random House, 1964. Contains "The World and the Jug," Ellison's famous reply to Howe's "Black Boys and Native Sons." Ellison criticizes Wright for overcommitting himself to political ideology and for employing restrictive naturalistic techniques.

Gayle, Addison. *The Way of the New World: The Black Novel in America.* Garden City, N.Y.: Doubleday, 1975. Gayle praises *Native Son* for its militant vision and argues that it provides a compelling model for future black writers.

Gloster, Hugh M. *Negro Voices in American Fiction.* Chapel Hill: University of North Carolina Press, 1948. Praises Wright for being the spokesman of the inarticulate masses of black people and regards *Native Son* as an important force in black literature, a "masterpiece of proletarian literature."

Howe, Irving. *A World More Attractive*. New York: Horizon, 1963. Contains "Black Boys and Native Sons," Howe's staunch defense of *Native Son* as a landmark work in American literature and culture. Howe praises the novel for its powerful rendering of truths that were skirted by earlier literature about blacks.

Smith, Valerie. *Self-Discovery and Authority in Afro-American Narrative*. Cambridge, Mass.: Harvard University Press, 1987. Draws revealing parallels between Richard Wright and Bigger Thomas in terms of their overcoming alienation by using language to counter the dehumanizing fictions imposed on them by a racist environment.

Collections of Essays

Abcarian, Richard. *Richard Wright's "Native Son": A Critical Handbook*. Belmont, Calif.: Wadsworth, 1970. A valuable research tool containing early reviews of *Native Son* and Wright's responses to some of them. It also contains essays by Wright, as well as a series of critical essays on the novel.

Bloom, Harold, ed. *Richard Wright's "Native Son."* New York, Chelsea House, 1988. A recent collection that includes many new articles on *Native Son*. Essays by Valerie Smith on the theme of alienation and by Joseph Skerrett on the composition of *Native Son* are particularly valuable.

Baker, Houston. *Twentieth Century Interpretations of "Native Son."* Englewood Cliffs, N.J.: Prentice-Hall, 1972. Features an excellent chronology of important dates in Wright's life and a rich selection of key essays, including work by McCall, Kent, Gibson, Howe, and Bone.

Fabre, Michel. *The World of Richard Wright*. Jackson: University of Mississippi Press, 1985. An invaluable collection of essays by Wright's most distinguished biographer. It includes previously published pieces on Wright's reading, his naturalism, and his exile in France. Also included are new essays on Wright's South and on Wright's interests in negritude and African literature.

Harper, Michael, and Robert Stepto. *Chant of Saints*. Urbana: University of Illinois Press, 1979. Contains Stepto's essay "I Thought I Knew These People: Richard Wright and the Afro-American Literary Tradition," a careful analysis of Wright's relationship to black culture and art.

Hakutani, Yoshinobu, ed. *Critical Essays on Richard Wright*. Boston: G. K. Hall, 1982. Contains an excellent introduction that provides an overview of Wright's career; seminal essays by Howe, Jackson, Kinnamon, Ellison, Hakutani, and Baker; and new essays by Reilly and Gibson.

Macksey, Richard, and Frank Moorer. *Richard Wright: A Collection of Critical Essays*. Englewood Cliffs, N.J.: Prentice-Hall, 1984. General essays on

Wright's importance, as well as criticism on *Native Son*. A special feature of this book is its series of articles focusing on Wright's existentialism.

Kinnamon, Keneth. *New Essays on Native Son*. Cambridge, England: Cambridge University Press, 1990. A fresh collection of essays on the fiftieth anniversary of the publication of *Native Son*. It includes Kinnamon's analysis of the composition and reception of the novel, John Reilly's discussion of how the novel subverts conventional American discourse on race, Trudier Harris's feminist interpretation, Houston Baker's New Historicist reading, and Craig Werner's discussion of the novel in terms of modernism and postmodernism.

Articles

Brivic, Sheldon. "Conflict of Values: Richard Wright's *Native Son*." *Novel* VII (Spring 1974): 231–45. Brivic refutes those critics who claim that *Native Son* is flawed by Wright's inadequate control of the ideas that inform the novel. He argues that Wright's ambivalent response to important political and social ideas adds to the richness of the novel and that Wright was well aware of the conflict of values at the center of his novel and dramatized this conflict powerfully to give a deeper, more enduring analysis of the dilemmas of American blacks.

Bryant, Jerry. "The Violence of *Native Son*." *Southern Review* 17 (April 1981): 303–19. Bryant sees Bigger Thomas as a representative modern man rather than a hero with a political vision. He turns to violence because society closes him off from positive areas of experience, yet even so, he is able, like Camus's Merseault, to achieve self-awareness leading to an existential identity.

Butler, Robert James. "Wright's *Native Son* and Two Novels by Zola: A Comparative Study." *Black American Literature Forum* 18 (Fall 1984): 100–05. Wright was deeply influenced by Zola's *La Bête humaine* and *Thérèse Racquin*, especially in terms of imagery, narrative structure, and characterization; however, Wright transformed materials from Zola in order to express his own unique vision as a black American.

———. "The Function of Violence in Richard Wright's *Native Son*." *Black American Literature Forum* 20 (Spring–Summer 1986): 9–25. Bigger's violent external action reflects the profound split in his character and also the pathological nature of his environment. By the end of the novel Bigger is able to transcend violence and imagine himself in human terms.

Emmanuel, James. "Fever and Feeling: Notes on the Imagery of *Native Son*." *Negro Digest* 18 (December 1968): 16–26. A careful study demonstrating that Bigger's psychological states are dramatized with images of light and dark, wall, curtains, and erasure.

Felgar, Robert. "The Kingdom of the Beast: The Landscape of *Native Son*." *CLA Journal* 17 (March 1974): 333–47. An analysis of Wright's conscious use of animal imagery to depict the white world's racist conceptions of blacks.

Gibson, Donald. "Wright's Invisible *Native Son*." *American Quarterly* 21 (Winter 1969): 728–39. A seminal essay arguing that critics misread *Native Son* because they fail to *see* its central character, mistaking him for the stereotypes the book consciously calls into question and transcends.

Hakutani, Yoshinobu. "*Native Son* and *An American Tragedy:* Two Different Interpretations of Crime and Guilt." *Centennial Review* 23 (Spring 1979): 208–26. Although the two novels are alike in ways that immediately catch the eye, a closer reading indicates that they are significantly different in structure, focus, and meaning.

Hernton, Calvin. "The Sexual Mountain and Black Women Writers." *Black American Literature Forum* 18 (Winter 1984): 139–45. Hernton uses *Native Son* as an illustration of his thesis that modern black literature has basically ignored the complexity of black feminine experience.

Jackson, Blyden. "Richard Wright: Black Boy from America's Black Belt and Urban Ghettos." *CLA Journal* 12 (June 1969): 387–323. An eloquent biographical essay arguing that all of Wright's major work is centered in his southern experiences.

Joyce, Joyce Ann. "Style and Meaning in Richard Wright's *Native Son*." *Black American Literature Forum* 16 (Summer 1982): 112–15. Wright was a scrupulous craftsman who used various rhetorical techniques effectively to create the sensation of anxiety and fear in *Native Son*.

Keady, Sylvia H. "Richard Wright's Women Characters and Inequality." *Black American Literature Forum* 10 (Winter 1976): 124–28. Wright's stereotyped portrayal of women reveals his pronounced sexist bias, which deeply flaws his fiction.

Kent, George E. "Richard Wright: Blackness and the Adventure of Western Culture." *CLA Journal* 12 (June 1969): 322–43. Kent argues that Wright's vision is centered in an ambivalence toward Western culture. On the one hand, Wright sees the West as offering the promise of individual liberty and social freedom; on the other hand, he deplores its history of racial oppression.

Kinnamon, Keneth. "Richard Wright's Use of *Othello* in *Native Son*." *CLA Journal* 12 (June 1969): 358–59. Similarities are pointed out between Mary Dalton and Desdemona, and the two death scenes are compared.

Nagel, James. "Images of 'Vision' in *Native Son*." *University Review* 35 (December 1969): 109–15. One of the novel's main image patterns centers on various forms of "blindness" the characters have toward one another as a result of their being conditioned by an impersonal, racist society.

Selected Bibliography

Pudaloff, Ross. "Celebrity as Identity: Richard Wright, *Native Son,* and Mass Culture." *Studies in American Fiction* 11 (Spring 1983): 3–18. A study of how Bigger's character is shaped in many ways by the movies, magazines, and detective stories that fascinated Wright.

Redden, Dorothy. "Richard Wright and *Native Son:* Not Guilty." *Black American Literature Forum* 10 (Winter 1976): 111–16. *Native Son* is not "choked with rage, hatred or vengefulness" but successfully transcends those feelings in moving toward a deeper understanding of racial problems in America.

Siegel, Paul. "The Conclusion of Richard Wright's *Native Son.*" *PMLA* 89 (May 1974): 517–23. A close reading of book 3 that disputes several previous interpretations of the novel's ending. Siegel provides a sympathetic view of Max and an apocalyptic interpretation of the novel, arguing that it ultimately cries out for a "third American revolution."

Tremaine, Louis. "The Dissociated Sensibility of Bigger Thomas in Wright's *Native Son.*" *Studies in American Fiction* 14 (Spring 1986): 63–76. A study of the deep split in Bigger's personality and Wright's use of expressionistic plotting, imagery, and point of view to dramatize this split.

Wertham, Frederic, M.D. "An Unconscious Determinant in *Native Son.*" *Journal of Clinical Psychopathology and Psychotherapy,* 6 (Winter 1944): 111–15. Demonstrates that certain traumatic episodes from Wright's early life, which were buried in his subconscious mind, found expression in *Native Son,* especially in scenes of violence.

Index

Index

The Author

Robert Butler received his Ph.D. in English from the University of Notre Dame in 1977. He is a professor of English and the director of College Honors at Canisius College in Buffalo, New York, and also teaches in the college program at Attica Correctional Facility. His research on black writers has resulted in the publication of numerous articles on Richard Wright, Ralph Ellison, Toni Morrison, and Alice Walker. He has also done extensive research in modern American fiction, publishing articles on Theodore Dreiser, John Dos Passos, James T. Farrell, Saul Bellow, and Erica Jong. He is currently at work on a book examining the journey motif in American literature from the turn of the century to the present.

He lives with his wife and four children in Tonawanda, New York.